ICME-13 Topical Surveys

Series editor

Gabriele Kaiser, Faculty of Education, University of Hamburg, Hamburg, Germany

More information about this series at http://www.springer.com/series/14352

Terezinha Nunes · Beatriz Vargas Dorneles
Pi-Jen Lin · Elisabeth Rathgeb-Schnierer

Teaching and Learning About Whole Numbers in Primary School

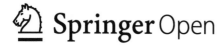

Terezinha Nunes
Department of Education
University of Oxford
Oxford
UK

Beatriz Vargas Dorneles
Universidade Federal do Rio Grande do Sul
Porto Alegre
Brazil

Pi-Jen Lin
Graduate Institute of Mathematics and
  Science Education
National Hsinchu University of Education
Hsinchu City
Taiwan

Elisabeth Rathgeb-Schnierer
University of Education Weingarten
Weingarten
Germany

ISSN 2366-5947   ISSN 2366-5955   (electronic)
ICME-13 Topical Surveys
ISBN 978-3-319-45112-1   ISBN 978-3-319-45113-8   (eBook)
DOI 10.1007/978-3-319-45113-8

Library of Congress Control Number: 2016948110

Printed on acid-free paper

This Springer imprint is published by Springer Nature
The registered company is Springer International Publishing AG Switzerland

Because we are incapable of grasping quantity directly by sight, we have invented numbers.

(Guedj 1998, p. 15)

Acknowledgments

The authors are grateful to the institutions and people who have contributed to the work reported here. Lee Hsiu-Fei from the National Taitung University, Taiwan, contributed with extensive work on a systematic review of papers related to teachers and teacher education, which was summarized here. The Nuffield Foundation funded a review of how children learn mathematics and some of the empirical work reported here. The views expressed here are the authors' own and do not represent the views of the Foundation.

Contents

Teaching and Learning About Whole Numbers in Primary School

1 Introduction

Our aim in this topical review of the teaching and learning of number was to search for pivotal ideas and domains of research that have occupied researchers in mathematics education within the last four decades and to draw some lessons for further research. We are aware that interest in mathematics education has existed for over 100 years, as documented by the founding of the journal *L'Enseignment Mathématique* in 1899 by Henri Fehr and Charles-Ange Laisant (Sriraman and English 2010), but we decided to focus on the last four decades of research because the research on the teaching and learning of number is plentiful and different approaches are clearly outlined. There was intensive activity in the design of New Math curricula in the 1950s and 1960s, which Sriraman and English viewed as an attempt "to change the mindless rigidity of traditional mathematics" (Sriraman and English 2010, p. 21). However, New Math met with much criticism from mathematicians. Among others, Freudenthal, in the first issue of *Educational Studies in Mathematics* and his welcome to the ICMI sponsored symposium on teaching mathematics so as to be useful, criticized the New Math movement for building a gap between mathematics and other disciplines: "People who apply mathematics often feel uneasy when observing that the mathematics they have been used to apply is replaced by something they judge less suited for applications" (Freudenthal 1968, p. 7). He speculated whether it would be necessary to wait a generation for those who apply mathematics to be reconciled with mathematics teaching. The New Math movement failed to become the mainstream mathematics curriculum in the long run, probably for a variety of reasons: it was not based on research on didactics or on learning; it was out of tune with the aims of previous curricula and the cultural expectations of what children should be taught; and it required a complete change in teacher education, to mention only a few. Nevertheless, it is possible that it had an impact on mathematics teaching and learning. The New Math movement cast doubt

© The Author(s) 2016
T. Nunes et al., *Teaching and Learning About Whole Numbers in Primary School*, ICME-13 Topical Surveys,
DOI 10.1007/978-3-319-45113-8_1

on the traditional teaching of arithmetic and helped to create a climate in which the study of mathematics education could flourish.

At the same time, Piaget's constructivism (Piaget 1950; 1953) was coming to the attention of mathematics education researchers. Gérard Vergnaud, one of Piaget's students, co-founded with Guy Brousseau the French society for the study of didactics of mathematics in the 1970s and wrote his theory of conceptual fields, which drew on Piaget's ideas and which has had a huge impact on mathematics education research. In the same year, the National Council of Teachers of Mathematics in the United States founded the *Journal for Research in Mathematics Education* (*JRME*) to provide more information on theoretical foundations and methods than was possible in the journals it already published, *Arithmetic Teacher* and *Mathematics Teacher* (Johnson 1970). Piaget's influence on the research published in the first 10 years of *JRME* is registered in some 20 papers that report research on conservation (Becher 1978; Callahan and Passi 1971; Carpenter and Lewis 1976; Carpenter 1975; Cathcart 1974; Gullen 1978; Huntington 1970; Kidder 1976; Mpiangu and Gentile 1975; Murray 1970; Owens and Steffe 1972; Peters 1970; Riggs and Nelson 1976; Romberg and Gilbert 1972; Schwebel and Schwebel 1974; Silver 1976; Sparks et al. 1970; Steffe and Carey 1972; Taloumis 1975, 1979). His influence on the establishment of mathematics education as an academic discipline is also documented in the recent account by Steffe of his personal trajectory (Lester and Steffe 2013). It is almost certain that other influences also contributed to the development of mathematics education research, but we will not examine them here, as our aim is not to trace the history of mathematics education but to give an indication of the intellectual climate in the decades that precede the review.

We do not report here a systematic review, but rather seek to identify ideas and their expression in mathematics education research. Some of these come from researchers in the domain itself, whereas others originate in psychology, owing largely to the influence of Piaget's theory and Vygotsky's emphasis on the role of cultural practices and cultural tools in the teaching and learning of scientific concepts. This survey cannot be exhaustive because research has been abundant and varied, but it can be used as a reference for those looking for a bird's eye view of research on teaching and learning about numbers. It is written for teachers and young researchers who are jumping onto a moving train.

The survey starts with a brief description of a theory of number meanings for teaching and learning that provides the basis for distinguishing the teaching and learning of arithmetic and problem solving, the theme of this review. For reasons of space, the review concentrates on whole numbers; rational numbers are not covered, in spite of the fact that they are a major stumbling block in primary school for both children and teachers. This is followed by an analysis of concepts and trends in teacher education for the teaching of number concepts. In the concluding section, we summarize the main points and raise questions for future research.

2 Survey on the State of the Art

2.1 A Theory of Number Meanings for Teaching and Learning

It is only natural to spend some time reflecting about the object of teaching—in this case, number—before a review of how it has been investigated in mathematics education. The theory of number meanings presented here, explained in Nunes and Bryant (2015), does not offer a new definition of number, but rather explores the meanings of number in the context of teaching primary school children. Without going into the philosophical divergences regarding the definition of cardinality, suffice it to say here that two aspects of Poincaré's (2013/1908) definition of whole numbers are taken on board: (a) the next number in the sequence of whole numbers is a whole number plus one; and (b) two numbers are equal if they are followed by the same next number.

These are crucial aspects for a theory of number meanings for teaching and learning because they emphasize from the start that there are relations between numbers in a number system and that therefore the definition of numbers and arithmetic are not independent of each other. They also invoke from the start an intuition of whole numbers as derived from addition, which in turn includes a reference to the real world: adding one does not mean literally adding the sign, but something for which the sign stands. One could oppose the use of intuition in a definition of number: Poincaré discussed this but eventually suggested that intuition cannot be discarded. In fact, he asserted that "the main aim of mathematics education is the development of certain capacities of the mind, and intuition is not the least important of these capacities. It is through intuition that mathematics remains in contact with the real world" (Poincaré 2013/1908, p. 76, our translation). Finally, this definition places number in the domain of signs: one, two, three etc. (in words or digits) are signs for something that is added to a number to obtain the next number. Numbers are signs for quantities.

Numbers and quantities are not the same thing. As Thompson (1993) suggested, one can think of quantities without representing them with a number; for example, one can say, "I have lots of books; he only has a few." One can reason about relations between quantities without representing them with numbers: Percy has more books than Susan and Susan has more books than Deborah; therefore, Percy has more books than Deborah. One can even quantify the relations between quantities by using numbers without representing the quantities themselves with numbers: Percy has 5 more books than Susan and Susan has 10 more books than Deborah; therefore, Percy has 15 more books than Deborah. This conclusion is possible only if one knows about the relations between numbers: 5 + 10 is 15, irrespective of what the numbers represent.

The use of numbers to represent quantities has consequences for mathematics education because the type of number that is used in representation depends on the type of quantity one wishes to represent. Even children aged six or seven understand that if four children share three chocolate bars, it is not possible for each one to receive a whole chocolate bar, but each one gets something. Some actually say that the quantity they get is not zero and it is not one, but they do not know a number to say how much each child will get (Mamede et al. 2005). Whole numbers represent quantities obtained by addition (or subtraction) of whole numbers; we need a different type of number to represent quantities obtained by division. To paraphrase Guedj, we need fractions, or more generally rational numbers, because we are incapable of grasping divisions of a whole into parts directly by sight.

We could explore these ideas in much more detail, but then we would not proceed to the review of research on teaching and learning about numbers. Where relevant, these ideas will be explored again. These brief examples illustrate that numbers have two types of meaning: a representational meaning, which refers to the use of numbers to represent quantities, and an analytical meaning, which is defined by a number system (Nunes and Bryant 2015). These different meanings of number provide a foundation for the distinction between arithmetic and quantitative reasoning, which is discussed in the subsequent section of this review.

2.2   Arithmetic and Quantitative Reasoning: Why They Are Different

When one thinks of numbers exclusively with respect to their analytical meaning, references to quantities are irrelevant: only the relations between numbers matter. Arithmetic is the study and use of relations between numbers to come to conclusions. Guedj (1998), who was Professor of History of Science at Paris VIII, defined arithmetic as "the science of numbers, which analyzes the behavior of various numbers in four operations: addition, subtraction, multiplication, and division" (Guedj 1998, p. 63). He considered arithmetic as the most difficult of the mathematical disciplines. Arithmetic includes calculating and much more: for example, it includes classifying numbers (e.g., odd and even numbers and primes and multiples), finding patterns in numerical operations (e.g., the sum of all consecutive numbers between 1 and 99 can be solved efficiently by finding a pattern that describes the addition of pairs of numbers, such as 1 and 99, 2 and 98, 3 and 97, etc., and figuring out how many of these pairs there are between 1 and 99), and analyzing conjectures (e.g., as Fermat did: can a perfect cube be the sum of two perfect cubes?). Guedj's concept of arithmetic is thus rather different from the concept often associated with primary school arithmetic, where arithmetic can be treated as learning to calculate, often by using memorized basic number facts (i.e., additions, subtractions, multiplications, and divisions of numbers up to 10) and by using algorithms that draw on knowledge of these number facts.

When the representational meaning of numbers comes into play, references to quantities are crucial. Quantitative reasoning (Thompson 1993) involves using numbers to represent quantities and relations between quantities as well as operating on the numbers to reach conclusions about the quantities. For some time mathematics education researchers have recognized the need to distinguish between arithmetic and problem solving: the distinction is inevitably connected to the need to go back to the real world in problem solving, which is not relevant to arithmetic. In this review we adopt the expression quantitative reasoning rather than problem solving because problems can emerge in different domains of mathematics and outside mathematics as well.

Carpenter et al. (1984) emphasized the significance of this distinction in a classic paper in which they analyzed the performance of 13-year-olds in a national assessment carried out in the United States. The researchers expressed concern not about the student's arithmetic, but about their quantitative reasoning. One of the problems given to the students was the following: An army bus holds 36 soldiers. If 1128 soldiers are being bused to their training site, how many buses are needed? They reported that about 70 % of the students performed the correct calculation, but about 29 % gave the exact quotient (31.33) as the answer and a further 18 % ignored the remainder. Carpenter et al. noted that those who gave the exact quotient response overlooked the fact that the number of buses should be a whole number (0.33 buses does not make sense); those who ignored the remainder failed to provide transportation for all the soldiers. Carpenter et al. emphasized that what is worrying about these answers is that the arithmetic is correct, but the quantitative reasoning is at fault: mathematics was being learned without a connection to meaning.

The importance of teaching mathematics in a way that keeps it connected to quantities in the world has been widely recognized. For example, the U.S. National Council of Teachers of Mathematics (NCTC), a professional organization dedicated to improving mathematics education, has consistently advocated the search for meaningful mathematics learning. It has launched several documents since its inception [e.g., the *Curriculum and Evaluation Standards for School Mathematics* (1989); the *Principles and Standards for School Mathematics* (2000); and the *Principles to Actions* (2013)] that have significantly influenced mathematics education standards worldwide. The recent document *Principles to Actions* urges the community of teachers to seek to attain excellence in teaching for all, and one of the means of achieving this is to avoid an excessive focus on learning procedures without any connection to meaning, understanding, or the applications that require these procedures.

In the Netherlands, Freudenthal (1971) argued that mathematics in the educational context must be seen as an activity of solving problems and looking for problems and not as a stock of rigid systems that were already organized in the past and now have to be learned. Researchers leading the center that later became known as the Freudenthal Institute coined the expression *mathematizing*, which means organizing reality in mathematically meaningful ways. Their investigations about teaching consistently start with activities that promote quantitative reasoning that are formalized over time. To use their terminology, teaching starts with horizontal mathematization, based on children's reasoning about quantities, which is followed by vertical mathematization, as formalization proceeds and connections to other mathematical representations and procedures are forged.

Thus there is broad agreement among mathematics education researchers that meaning is important. However, as one can see in the subsequent section, the interpretation of what meaning is in the context of teaching children about number varies, because numbers have two types of meaning, an analytical meaning and a representational meaning. Some teaching approaches focus only on the analytical meaning of numbers and others comprise the representational meaning as well as the analytical meaning.

2.3   Teaching Arithmetic in Primary School

2.3.1   Teaching and Learning Arithmetic Using Written Algorithms

Arithmetic is always carried out using a number system, which has specific characteristics. In this review, we do not discuss different types of number systems, a topic which could take up the whole of the review and has been masterfully analyzed in other publications (e.g., Lancy 1983; Lean 1992; Miller and Stigler 1987; Miura et al. 1988; Owens 2001; Saxe 1981; Seron and Fayol 1994; Zaslavsky 1999). We focus on arithmetic carried out with either an oral or a written numeration system that uses place value notation, because place value notation is widely adopted around the world today. We start with a section that focuses on research on written arithmetic, which has been an object of intense research effort since the early 1980s, and move on to other approaches to the study of arithmetic competence, which gained more importance later on.

Research with a focus on the teaching and learning of addition and subtraction using the traditional computational algorithms is clearly justified: many curricula in different parts of the world aim to teach these algorithms as an efficient way of calculating. At the same time, many children find it difficult to learn the written algorithms when carrying and borrowing are involved. A search for research on multi-digit addition and subtraction yields a vast number of papers that cannot be reviewed in detail. However, clear lessons have been learned from this work, which we summarize here.

First, quantitative and qualitative methods have abundantly documented children's difficulties in learning multi-digit addition and subtraction (Brown and Burton 1978; Brown and VanLehn 1982; Carpenter et al. 1998; Fuson 1990a, b; Hennessy 1994; Hiebert and Wearne 1996; Nunes Carraher and Schlieman 1985; Nunes Carraher et al. 1985; Resnick 1982; Selter 2001; Young and O'Shea 1981). Qualitative analyses suggested that children's difficulties could be described in a variety of ways: a weak understanding of place value, a disconnection between their understanding of a base-10 number system and the syntax of the computational rules taught in schools, the implementation of faulty procedures resulting from pedagogical obstacles created by learning rules such as "you can't take a larger number from a smaller number" (so you just take the smaller number from the bigger one), and a lack of conservation of the minuend in subtraction (e.g., children borrow from one column but forget to reduce the value appropriately).

We exemplify here the implementation of faulty procedures, or "bugs in the algorithm," as they were termed by Brown and VanLehn (1982), with three examples:

(1) Smaller-from-larger: For example, when calculating 226 − 38, the student obtains the answer 212 by taking 6 away from 8 and 2 away from 3.
(2) Difference 0: When the minuend has a 0, the student writes down the aligned digit from the subtrahend, because any number minus 0 is the same number; for example, 200 − 35 = 200.
(3) Borrow from zero: when facing a subtraction such as 407 − 8, the student obtains 499, by subtracting 8 from 17, correctly borrowing and adding to the ones column, making the 0 into a 9 because 1 had been borrowed from the tens column, but forgetting that something had been borrowed from the hundreds column.

These are common examples and certainly well known to primary school teachers. Many others can be described. The reason Brown and VanLehn (1982) termed these errors bugs in the algorithm is that they are not simply a result of lack of attention or a whim; they seem to be systematic rules used by the same children across examples and by quite a few children too (for a different view, see Hennessy 1994).

Second, the quantitative and qualitative results from research on multi-digit addition and subtraction, which suggested that children were learning rules in a meaningless fashion, reinforced the concerns about teaching for meaning in mathematics education. Thus, much subsequent research focused on teaching children about place value more explicitly, using different sorts of concrete materials to help children understand the connection between place value and the quantities represented by digits (e.g., Baroody 1990; Fuson 1990a, b; Fuson and Briars 1990; Ho and Cheng 1997; Resnick 1983). The interpretation of meaning here is restricted to the analytical meaning of number. Children were taught to manipulate the materials used to represent place value in restricted ways so that they could learn how to manipulate the numbers.

Research on teaching multi-digit addition and subtraction using manipulatives to represent ones, tens, and hundreds was seen as justified by Bruner's (1966) theory of instruction. Bruner is known for having asserted that any subject can be taught effectively in some intellectually honest form to any child at any stage of development. His theory proposed that children first learn things using enactive (i.e., in action) representations; later they become able to use iconic representations (representations through visual means) and finally they are able to use symbolic representations. The materials used in studies included base-10 blocks (in which ones are represented by small cubes, tens are represented by bars made of 10 small cubes, and hundreds by squares with 10 by 10 cubes), unifix blocks (single cubes that can be attached to form blocks of tens) or sticks (tied in bundles of tens, which can be tied into 10 bundles to form 100). These items provide iconic representations for children to learn about place value.

Some researchers concluded that this approach showed some degree of success (Fuson and Briars 1990; Fuson et al. 1997; Ross 1989) at least with children from second grade onwards, but criticisms were also raised. Cobb (1987) and Gravemeijer et al. (1990) suggested that perhaps it is necessary to have the concept of "ten" already within the number system in order to appreciate what the tens rods mean.

At any rate, the use of manipulatives to represent ones, tens, and hundreds was an attempt to give meaning to the written digits by focusing on the analytic meaning of numbers, not to take advantage of the representational meaning of numbers by connecting them to quantities. The relation between the numbers and the quantities they represented was not the focus of this research endeavor. In fact, the results of many subtractions where bugs in the algorithm existed were numbers which could not possibly be correct if the students thought about the quantities: how could one take 8 from 407 and end up with 499?

Research on the teaching of written algorithms as well as on the loss of meaning after their correct implementation led many researchers started to query when the standard algorithms should be taught (Baroody 1990) or actually whether to teach them at all (Carroll 1996). A focus on children's own methods or alternative ways of teaching, such as the use of the empty number line and mental arithmetic, became part of research as well as recognized items in the curriculum in primary school in different countries (Ashcroft and Fierman 1982; Anghileri 2001; Beishuizen 1993; Beishuizen et al. 1997; Beishuizen and Klein 1998; Bramald 2000; Bobis 2007; Fuson and Burghardt 2013; Ginsburg 1977; Gravemeijer 1993; Groen and Resnick 1977; Klein et al. 1998; Murphy 2011; Torbeyns et al. 2009b; Thompson 2000; Torbeyns et al. 2009c; Van den Heuvel-Panhuizen 2008). Thus new themes appear in research on arithmetic in mathematics education after the research on teaching written algorithms: mental arithmetic [which is not new in the curriculum; according to Shulmann (1986) it appeared in the California State Board examination for elementary school teachers from March 1875] and flexibility.

2.3.2   Teaching and Learning Mental Arithmetic

Mental calculation means that arithmetic problems are solved mentally without using a written standard procedure. While standard written procedures focus on calculation with single digits (the ones, the tens, the hundreds, etc.), the process of mental calculation with whole numbers (Krauthausen 1993) is more complex (especially with multi-digit numbers) and requires a deep understanding of number and of relations between operations as well as knowledge of basic facts and fact families (Heirdsfield and Cooper 2004; Threlfall 2002).

Mental calculation strategies for multi-digit addition and subtraction have been categorized in various ways (see e.g., Carpenter et al. 1997; Fuson et al. 1997;

Klein et al. 1998; Thompson 1999; Threlfall 2002) using different names and different numbers of categories (three to five). Criteria for classification have been defined as splitting up numbers into tens and ones (both numbers or only one number) and as rounding and compensating. German researchers, as well as most German text books, rely on six main categories of mental strategies for addition and subtraction (Selter 2001):

- jump strategy, characterized by splitting up one number and keeping together the second one (56 + 28 = 56 + 20 + 8);
- split strategy in which both numbers get split into tens and ones (56 + 28 = 50 + 20 + 6 + 8);
- mix of split and jump (56 + 28, 50 + 20 = 70, 76 + 8);
- compensation strategy in which one number gets rounded (56 + 28 = 56 + 30 − 2);
- simplifying strategy, characterized by modifying the problem without changing the result (56 + 28 = 54 + 30); and
- indirect addition (only for subtraction problems) (72 − 69, 69 + 3 = 72).

The six categories just described represent idealized types of strategies and do not reflect individual variations for solving a problem (Threlfall 2002). Thus, these categories are helpful in analyzing students' solutions generally, but they are not sufficient to give a deep insight into individual processes of solving a calculation.

Rathgeb-Schnierer (2011) proposed a model for describing the process of mental calculation in detail, with distinct but interrelated dimensions that have different functions and different degrees of explication. Figure 1 identifies these elements as (1) methods of calculation, (2) cognitive elements, and (3) tools for solution (Rathgeb-Schnierer 2011; Rathgeb-Schnierer and Green 2013).

The dimension *methods of calculation* (see Fig. 1) includes the three general ways any given problem can be solved: (1) by using the standard algorithm (2) by combining mental calculation with whole numbers and notation (e.g. partial sums or methods with students' idiosyncratic notations), and (3) through mental

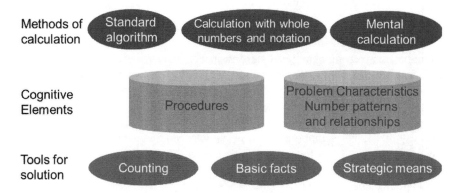

Fig. 1 Dimensions of mental calculation process (Rathgeb-Schnierer and Green 2013, p. 354)

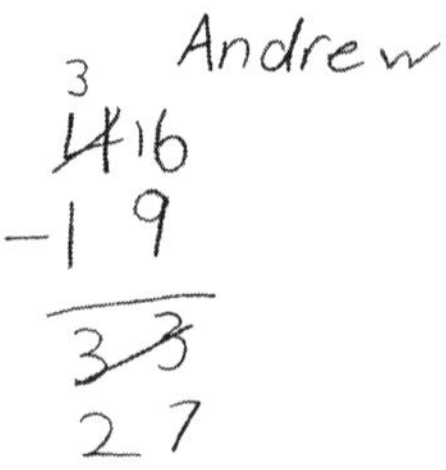

Fig. 2 Andrew (second
grader) solves 46 – 19

calculation alone. Methods of calculation can sometimes be directly observed but do not provide information about how an answer is determined.

Andrews' notation (Fig. 2), for example, suggests that he relied on a standard algorithm to solve 46 – 19. Although the minuend and the subtrahend are written correctly, it is not obvious how he figured out the difference in each column separately, because this was not part of the observable behavior but was carried out mentally. Regarding the column of the ones, there were many possible tools for solution that could be have led to the difference between 16 and 9, such as counting up or back, drawing on basic facts, or using adaptive strategic means (e.g., 16 + 1 – 9 + 1 or 17 – 10). The method of calculation by itself does not reveal the mental processes that lead to the solution of a computation.

Andrews' notation makes it clear that he used a standard algorithm, but it does not provide any information about two aspects: Firstly, how he obtained the solution in each column, and, secondly, why he discovered that his first approach, which led to the answer 33, was not correct. There are several possibilities: he could have estimated that the answer had to be less than 30 (40 minus almost 20 has to be less than 30), he could have checked the answer by adding and estimating (33 plus almost 20 should be about 50), or he could have counted up from 33 and found that he got to 41 more quickly than expected.

A second dimension in mental calculation refers to cognitive elements. Veronika (2nd grader) exemplifies this domain in solving 71 – 36.

Veronika: Um [looks at the problem 71 – 36], I do 71 minus 30 equals 41, and then minus 1 equals 40, and then there is minus 5 equals 35.

Veronika shows a "begin with one number method" (Fuson et al. 1997) by decomposing the subtrahend and subtracting it step by step. The tools she used for solving seem to rely on a combination of basic facts and strategic means, composing, and decomposing. However, one cannot tell whether her solution derives from a learned procedure, from the recognition and use of number patterns and relations, or from a combination of both. Consequently, for a correct assessment of Veronika's abilities in mental math, it would be helpful to know which cognitive elements came into play during her solution process. In the Rathgeb-Schnierer and Green (2013) model of process of calculation, cognitive elements are defined as specific mental experiences that sustain the learning process. These can be learned *procedures* (such as computing algorithms) or recognition of *number characteristics* (such as number patterns and relations). In reality, it is difficult to reconstruct the basic cognitive elements that lie behind an overt solution process. Looking at Veronika's solution, it is not clear whether she followed a procedural solution conducted mentally but mechanically or recognized the number characteristics and based her solution on number knowledge and number sense. In order to describe her mental calculation abilities more precisely, it would be critical to know which cognitive elements her solution entails.

Cognitive elements are not sufficient to find the answer to a computation; they rely on additional tools that are used and combined in the given context to solve the problem. The specific tools for solution may involve counting, referring to basic facts, or employing adaptive strategic means (Rathgeb-Schnierer and Green 2013). Strategic means are devices that modify complex problems to make them easier. Such strategic means can be combined in flexible ways and include, for example, decomposing and composing $(65 + 28 = 60 + 20 + 5 + 5 + 3)$, transforming a problem $(46 - 19 = 47 - 20)$, deriving the solution from a known problem (if 7 joined with 7 equals 14, the answer to 7 joined with 8 equals 15, since 8 is one more than 7), and using decade analogies (if 4 joined with 5 is 9, 40 joined with 50 must be 90).

Whenever an arithmetic problem is solved, all three dimensions are involved. Thus the model can be used as a theoretical framework to analyze students' solution processes and to identify their mental competences. The fruitfulness of the use of the model as an analytic frame is exemplified in the analysis of Michael's solution of the subtraction problem $71 - 36$:

Michael: Okay, here [picks card with the problem $71 - 36$]. Now I do 70 minus 35 and then I know the answer immediately: it's 35
Interviewer: Why do you know the answer immediately?
Michael: Because then I have [points at the number 36] – 35, and 35 is half of 70, and then here [points at the number 71] I have 70.

Michael has solved the problem mentally (method for calculation) by transforming the actual problem into a new one that preserves the difference between the numbers. The transformed problem seems to be almost trivial for him because he found the answer immediately. Michael's solution relied on a combination of (1) strategic means (transforming the numbers but keeping the difference the same) and (2) known facts (35 is half of 70). The transformation and argumentation suggest that Michael has not referred to a learned procedure but to numerical relations and special characteristics of the problem (numerical proximity and half/double). He has used and combined tools for solution according to this specific subtraction problem; his approach to solve the computation emerged during the process and was unique for that specific situation. Michael recognized the numerical proximity of 71 to 70 and adapted this knowledge to the situation by transforming the problem.

Although the term mental arithmetic is widely adopted in research and teaching, some researchers have suggested an alternative description. Nunes et al. (1993) prefer the contrast between written and oral arithmetic rather than written and mental arithmetic. Each of these forms of arithmetic uses a different medium: written or oral number systems. In either form, mental manipulations of numbers are implemented based on mentally stored information about relations between numbers. The most striking findings of the studies on oral arithmetic are that (1) this practice often emerges among groups with limited or no schooling in the context of their occupations; (2) calculation is very flexible, using different moves that are appropriate for the context; (3) oral arithmetic refers to quantities, not to written symbols; and (4) oral arithmetic is accurate in the absence of higher levels of written calculation skill (Gay and Cole 1967; Reed and Lave 1981; Moll et al. 1984; Nunes et al. 1993).

Nunes et al. (1993) described the properties of operations that support oral arithmetic and the variety of procedures in detail. Oral addition and subtraction rely on the associative property of these operations; multiplication and division rely on the distributive property of multiplication with respect to addition and of division with respect to subtraction. Multiplication often uses doubling and division uses halving when these facilitate the process. All four operations often make the use of the inverse operation during calculation. We transcribe below two examples of calculation using oral arithmetic that illustrate the references to quantities rather than to digits and the use of maneuvers which are not part of written arithmetic. Both children were in third grade.

> R: I have 243 cruzeiros (the Brazilian currency at the time) in my pocket. I want to buy this bag of marbles. You are selling the bag for 75 cruzeiros. How much money will I have left?
>
> C: You just give me the two hundred [he seems to have meant 100 or changed his mind]. I'll give you 25 back. Plus the 43 that you have, the 143, that's 168 (Nunes et al. 1993, p. 41). [The decomposition of 200 into 100 + 143 is unusual in comparison to written arithmetic.]
>
> R: You have 75 marbles, to distribute fairly to five boys. How many marbles will each one get?
>
> C: If you give 10 marbles to each [child], that's 50 [marbles]. There are 25 left over. To distribute to five boys, 25, that's hard. [R: That's a hard one.] That's five more each. Fifteen each (Nunes et al. 1993, p. 43). [The references to the quantities, boys, and marbles, although implicit at times, are clear in the transcript; each is always a reference to the boys.]

Nunes (2002) argued that the use of cultural tools such as number systems is necessary for arithmetic and that the tools both enable and constrain people's reasoning. Number systems are necessary because without a number system that defines relations between numbers, arithmetic is not possible. However, the influence of a particular system on a person's reasoning is more subtle. When one uses an oral number system, we say the hundreds, then the tens, and then the ones. Nunes et al. (1993) describe a plethora of examples of oral arithmetic in settings in which written arithmetic is used, such as calculations by vendors in street markets and by foremen and fishermen in the course of their work. The direction of calculation in oral arithmetic is invariably in line with this way of enunciating numbers: hundreds, tens, and ones. In contrast, when people write down a number, they can operate in the opposite direction and separate by ones, tens, and hundreds.

In this process, number meaning is often lost, and errors such as those described by Brown and VanLehn (1982) are not necessarily recognized by the person doing the calculation. The effect of different oral systems of signs on children's interpretation of number and on their arithmetic skills has also been recognized in research in mathematics education (e.g., Bender and Beller 2011; Chung and Bryant 2001; Fuson and Kwon 1992; Miller et al. 1995, 2000; Miller and Stigler 1987; Miura et al. 1999; Song and Ginsburg 1988). An aspect that has not been explored systematically in the research described in this and in the subsequent section is the form of presentation of the calculation tasks; this might turn out to be more important than it appears and could be a new aspect for investigation in the future.

2.3.3 Flexibility in Mental Calculation

Definitions of flexibility in mental calculation have varied among researchers. This has led to multiple and sometimes inconsistent perspectives on the concept (Star and Newton 2009). These varying definitions have resulted in different ways of operationalizing the concept (see, for example, Verschaffel et al. 2009; Torbeyns et al. 2009a; Selter 2009; Threlfall 2002; Rathgeb-Schnierer and Green 2013). There has been some consensus among all the definitions on the idea that flexibility in mental calculation includes two central features: the knowledge of different solution methods and the ability to adapt them appropriately when solving a problem. However, it is exactly in this respect that crucial differences in the definitions emerge. Based on various definitions, Threlfall (2009) identified two different explanatory models for flexibility in mental calculation: one based on the idea of conscious or unconscious strategic choice and one based on the idea of "zeroing in" on a solution based on number knowledge and conceptual understanding.

Rechtsteiner-Merz (2013) systematically analyzed the various notions of flexibility in the literature and identified three different approaches regarding what is meant by the adaptive use of strategies and how this can be identified: (1) appropriateness of solution path and task characteristics, (2) accuracy and speed, and (3) appropriateness of cognitive elements that sustain the solution process. Each of these is explained in turn.

(1) Appropriateness of solution method and task characteristics: This notion emphasizes the match between solution method and specific task characteristics. It is based on the assumption that there is one most suitable solution method for each specific task, and that this method is chosen consciously or unconsciously (see e.g., Blöte et al. 2000; Klein et al. 1998; Star and Newton 2009).

(2) Accuracy and speed: One research group (Torbeyns et al. 2009a) enhanced its definition of flexibility and operationalized flexibility (adequacy) in terms of correctness and speed of obtaining a solution.

(3) Appropriateness of cognitive elements that sustain the solution process: Researchers who adopt this approach do not share the idea of choice between different solution paths (see, e.g., Threlfall 2002, 2009; Rathgeb-Schnierer 2010; Rathgeb-Schnierer and Green 2013, 2015). Rather than the choice of the most suitable solution or the quickest way of obtaining a solution, appropriateness is conceived as a match between the combination of strategic means and the recognition of number patterns and relations of a given problem during the computation process. The recognition of number patterns and relations and their use in solving a computation depends on a student's knowledge of numbers and operations. In this sense, flexibility in mental calculation can be considered as an "interaction between noticing and knowledge" (Threlfall 2002, p. 29).

All three approaches to mental flexibility can be linked to the model proposed for the process of calculation presented in Fig. 1. The first two approaches focus predominantly on a single domain of the calculation process: either the domain methods of calculation or the domain tools for solution. Within the third approach, researchers also take the cognitive elements into account and therefore focus on two different domains to identify the degree of flexibility in students' mental arithmetic: solution methods and the cognitive elements that sustain the solution processes. Consequently, evidence of flexibility in mental calculation can exist only if the tools for solution are linked in a dynamic way to problem characteristics, number patterns, and relationships.

Different methods have been used in the study of flexibility in mental calculation, some of which, such as the choice/no-choice method, borrowed from other domains of research where decision making is involved. We single out the choice/no-choice method for description here, as it may lead to other uses of the method in different contexts in mathematics education. The paradigm is simple: in the choice condition, the participants are allowed to solve the task in whichever way they desire. In the no-choice condition, participants are shown a demonstration of the method they should use in the task. Using this methodology, Verschaffel and his colleagues have been able to demonstrate that some of the assumptions made about what is the best strategy for some tasks might be questionable. When students are taught different ways of approaching subtraction, for example, they are encouraged to use subtraction by complementary addition in tasks where the difference between the minuend and the subtrahend is small; it is assumed that in tasks where the difference between the minuend and the subtrahend is large, direct subtraction is more efficient. However, using the choice/no-choice method, they observed that children (Verschaffel et al. 2016) as well as adults (Torbeyns et al. 2009c, 2011) are faster and more accurate when they use complementary addition as the route to solving subtraction problems, irrespective of whether the difference between the minuend and the subtrahend is large or small.

Based on different definitions of flexibility and on different methods, researchers have examined different elements of flexibility in mental addition and subtraction and reported a variety of results:

- After learning the standard computation algorithms, students prefer them and do not utilize previously learned strategies, even when the latter continue to be more advantageous and appropriate (Selter 2001).
- When students learn through examples, they tend to learn specific procedures rather than general rules or relationships; this has a negative impact on the development of mental flexibility (Klein et al. 1998; Heirdsfield and Cooper 2004; Schütte 2004).
- Students' strategies depend on different factors, such as the target operation (Torbeyns et al. 2009a), specific problem characteristics (Blöte et al. 2000; Torbeyns et al. 2009a), and student-initiated recognition of problem characteristics (Rathgeb-Schnierer 2006, 2010).
- Students who exhibit flexible and adaptive expertise in mental calculation also show deep understanding of number and operation relationships as well as knowledge of basic facts and fact families. These students also possess high self-confidence and a positive attitude towards mathematics (Heirdsfield and Cooper 2002, 2004; Hope 1987; Threlfall 2002). Additionally they are able to recognize and to use of number patterns and relationships to solve problems (Rathgeb-Schnierer 2006, 2010; Schütte 2004; Threlfall 2009).
- The development of flexibility in mental calculation can be supported by special approaches to mathematics education. In this regard researchers have highlighted the problem-solving approach in general (Heinze et al. 2009; Grüßing et al. 2013) combined with specific activities for fostering number sense. Rechtsteiner-Merz and Rathgeb-Schnierer (2015) have developed and investigated a special instructional approach with activities that encourage students to focus on number patterns, problem characteristics, and numerical and structural relationships (the approach is called "*Zahlenblickschulung*," which literally means "training of number sight").
- Students with low achievement in mathematics need special instructional approaches to develop flexibility in mental calculation (Verschaffel et al. 2007). The "*Zahlenblickschulung*" approach supports the development of knowledge of numerical relations and conceptual knowledge, which is the fundamental condition for the development of calculation strategies and flexible mental calculation (Rechtsteiner-Merz 2013).

Recent studies reported in the field of flexible mental calculation reflect not only different interests and aims, but also different definitions of flexibility, which influence both the research methods used and data interpretation. These various definitions of flexibility also lead to different emphases in teaching, with the aim of promoting flexibility in mental calculation (Selter 2009; Threlfall 2009). According to Threlfall, "The assumption that it is all a matter of strategic choice will lead to very different conclusions about appropriate action from the perspective that presumes the importance of conceptual understanding and thinks of some kind of calculating as 'zeroing in' on solutions" (2009, p. 552). The two distinct assumptions lead naturally to two approaches to teaching towards flexibility: (1) different strategies are taught, and student discussions are encouraged; (2) teachers support the development of conceptual understanding that includes a deep knowledge about numbers and relations between numbers.

In short, flexibility in mental calculation has become an important topic in primary mathematics education throughout the last decade, and substantial research has been reported in the field. However, there is little empirical evidence so far about the development of flexibility in mental calculation and the effects of instructional approaches. In this context it would be important for further research to focus on the description of the development of flexibility in mental calculation (regarding all operations), the identification of individual and general factors which influence the development of flexibility in mental calculation, the identification of obstacles for the development of flexibility in mental calculation, and the identification of supportive instructional approaches.

2.4   Quantitative Reasoning in Primary School

Thompson (1993) defined quantitative reasoning as:

> the analysis of a situation into a quantitative structure—a network of quantities and quantitative relationships. A prominent characteristic of reasoning quantitatively is that numbers and numeric relationships are of secondary importance, and do not enter into the primary analysis of a situation. What is important is relationships among quantities. In that regard, quantitative reasoning bears a strong resemblance to the kind of reasoning customarily emphasized in algebra instruction. (Thompson 1993, p. 186)

This clear definition is very helpful because it helps separate out quantitative reasoning from arithmetic. Whereas arithmetic is based on relations between numbers, quantitative reasoning is based on relations between quantities; their measures, i.e., the numbers used to represent the quantities, are of secondary importance.

Substantial efforts were invested in research in the 1980s in the analysis of the quantitative relations that define different types of problems that children are expect to master in mathematics education in primary school. Two types of quantitative relations were identified through such analyses: additive and multiplicative reasoning. Additive reasoning is based on quantities connected by part-whole relations; multiplicative reasoning is based on quantities connected by one-to-many correspondences or ratios (Nunes and Bryant 1996, 2015). This classification simplifies significantly the analysis of the types of quantitative reasoning tasks and offers a great contribution to curriculum design. Each of these schemas of reasoning was considered in detail by several authors in order to define different types of problems. This section first considers research on additive reasoning and subsequently research on multiplicative reasoning.

2.4.1 Additive Reasoning

Additive reasoning in primary school was investigated in a very large number of studies (e.g., Carpenter et al. 1981; Carpenter and Moser 1982; De Corte and Verschaffel 1985, 1987; Ginsburg 1982; Hudson 1983; Nesher 1982; Stern 1993; Svenson and Broquist 1975; Vergnaud 1979, 1982; to cite just a few). In the domain of additive reasoning, such considerable consensus emerged with respect to this classification that Romberg (1982) defined this classification as an emergent paradigm for research on addition and subtraction. Three different types of situations that involve part-whole relations have been identified.

1. Situations that involve transformations: For example, "Paul had 16 stamps. He gave 5 away. How many does he have now?" The transformations can be additive or subtractive, as in the example just presented. The unknown in the problem can be the starting point, the transformation, or the result. Thus situations that involve transformations can give origin to six different types of problems, by combining each type of transformation with each position of the unknown.
2. Situations that involve composition of two quantities: For example, "Jasmin has 4 red and 9 gold fish in her fishbowl. How many fishes does she have in the fishbowl?" There are only two possible types of problems in composition situations: either the total is missing or one of the parts is missing.
3. Situations that involve comparison relations: For example, "Alex has 13 books and Camilla has 8 books. How many more books does Alex have than Camilla?" The unknown in comparison situations can be the comparative relation (5 in this case), the reference set ("Alex has some books; he has 5 more books than Camilla. Camilla has 8 books. How many books does Alex have?") or the compared set ("Alex has 13 books. He has 5 more books than Camilla. How many books does Camilla have?").

Research in this domain has led to convergent conclusions across studies in different countries, which we summarize here.

First, different rates of correct responses have been found for problems that require the same arithmetic calculation. For example, in transformation situations, problems with the result unknown have been shown to be significantly easier than those in which the starting point is unknown. Another consistent result has been that, when the situation involves the composition of two quantities, finding the whole has been consistently easier than finding a part. Problems that involve comparisons have been the most difficult of all; they have been shown to be particularly difficult if the unknown in the problem has been the reference set. An inescapable conclusion from such results is that quantitative reasoning has indeed been shown to be different from arithmetic: if the arithmetic computation was controlled for and the quantitative reasoning demands varied, the rates of correct responses varied with the quantitative reasoning demands.

Second, some additive reasoning situations involved just quantities whereas others involved quantities and relations. If a problem required reasoning about relations, it was significantly more difficult than a similar one that involved just quantities. For example, Hudson (1983) asked first grade children in the United States to answer problems that had the same number of pieces of information; the information was presented in some problems only in terms of quantities, and in others it was presented as quantities and relations. For example, a quantities-only problem was: "The birds are racing to get the worms (the children saw a card with birds and worms). There are six birds and four worms. How many birds won't get worms?" The problem with quantities and relations was: "The birds are racing to get the worms (the children saw a card with birds and worms). There are six birds and four worms. How many more birds than worms?" The first graders were 100 % correct when answering the first type of question and 64 % correct when answering the second type of question.

Third, students' concepts of arithmetic operations must change over time for them to make progress on quantitative reasoning. Vergnaud (1979) hypothesized that young children had a concept of addition based on the schema of action of joining sets. This schema was useful for solving problems that involved transformation of a quantity by addition or problems that involved the composition of quantities into a single whole. However, this concept was insufficient for solving problems in a transformation situation in which the quantity decreases but the starting point was unknown (e.g. "Paul had some stamps. He gave 5 to Simon and now he has 8 stamps. How many did he have before he gave stamps to Simon?"). To solve this start-unknown problem, addition must be conceived as the inverse of subtraction. In a classic study, Hart et al. (1985; see also Brown 1981a, b) documented the difficulty that 11- to 13-year-olds have in conceiving of subtraction as the inverse of addition. The problem the students were asked to solve was: "The Green family have to drive 261 miles to get from London to Leeds. After driving 87 miles they stop for lunch. How do you work out how far they still have to drive?" The students' task was simply to mark the correct computation that could be entered in a calculator to find the answer. Only 60 % of the 11- and 12-year-olds and 67 % of the 13-year-olds chose the correct solution. Their difficulty cannot be attributed to arithmetic problems, as they did not have to calculate the answer. Thus it must be related to a restricted concept of subtraction, which did not include the idea of subtraction as the inverse of addition.

Verschaffel (1994) analyzed the difficulty of comparison problems which require an analogous inverse reasoning, but applied to relations rather than operations. In a comparison problem, a relation can be described as "more than" but the students must think of its inverse to solve the problem if the compared set is the missing information (e.g., "Pete has 29 nuts. He has 14 more nuts than Rita. How many nuts does Rita have?"). He asked fifth graders in Belgium (aged about 11 years) to solve comparison problems in which the relation was consistent with the operation (i.e., the relation was described as "more than" and the operation to be used to solve the problem was an addition) or was inconsistent (i.e., the relation was described as "more than" and the operation to be used to solve the problem was a subtraction, as in the problem presented above). When the relation and the operation were consistent, 92.5 % of the responses were correct; when the relation and the operation were inconsistent, 72.5 % of the responses were correct. Thus students must learn not only that addition can be conceived as the inverse of subtraction and vice versa, but also that the relation "more than" can be conceived as the inverse of "less than" and vice versa.

Thompson (1993) rightly pointed out that much of the research on additive reasoning includes only three pieces of information, usually either (1) two quantities connected by a transformation, (2) two quantities combined into a total quantity, or (3) two quantities and a relation between them. He explored the difficulty of problems that had structures different from these basic ones but still used the same part-whole relations. In his problems, there was typically more information, and some of the information about quantities had to be deduced from the information about relations. We have no quantitative data from his studies, and space does not permit the inclusion of his fascinating qualitative descriptions. Thus we provide quantitative information from a study by Nunes et al. (2015), who gave a quantitative reasoning assessment to a sample of over 1000 students in the age range 10–11 years in England. A problem that involved four quantities and three relations was: "Kate, Donna, and Jamie shared some stickers between them. Altogether they bought 22 stickers. Donna got 3 more than Kate and Jamie got 4 more than Kate. How many did each of them have?" It was noted that all the relations here were additive. The value of only one quantity is given: the total number of stickers. The value of the parts is not given, only the relations between the parts. The arithmetic required to solve this problem is quite simple, but the web of relations between the quantities is complex because the quantities of stickers that Donna and Jamie had were described in relation to the quantity that Kate had. This problem was solved correctly by only 31 % of the students.

The inescapable conclusion from the brief review of studies carried out here is that one must indeed distinguish arithmetic from quantitative reasoning. The level of difficulty of problems cannot be described by the difficulty of the arithmetic calculations. Quantitative reasoning must become part of the themes addressed in mathematics education curricula. Moreover, quantitative reasoning cannot be conceived simply as the application of procedures learned to solve arithmetic computations. Additive reasoning develops throughout the primary school years (Thompson 1993; Vergnaud 1979, 1982) and must be seen as a domain of teaching and learning on its own; students need to learn to reason about relations between quantities in order to solve problems, not only about arithmetic. Before we turn to research about teaching quantitative reasoning, we consider research on multiplicative reasoning.

2.4.2   Multiplicative Reasoning

There has been less convergence on the classification of problem types in multiplicative reasoning, but there has been agreement with respect to the fact that multiplicative relations differ from additive relations: additive relations are part-whole relations, whereas multiplicative relations are based on ratios (i.e., one-to-many correspondences). The classification presented here is based on Nunes and Bryant (1996, 2008, 2015), who attempted a synthesis of the different classifications of multiplicative reasoning situations.

1. Situations that involve a direct ratio between two quantities: For example, one lorry has four wheels, one kilo of fish costs 15 dollars, etc. These problems have received different names in the research literature, such as composite-unit problems, isomorphism of measure, or one-to-many correspondence problems (Becker 1993; Kaput 1985; Kaput and West 1994; Steffe 1994; Vergnaud 1982). These problems are solved by multiplication or division, depending on which quantity is unknown. When the unit value is given, there are three types of problems: multiplication (e.g., Each child who comes to our party will receive 3 balloons and 8 children are coming. How many balloons do we need?), partitive division (e.g., We have 24 balloons and 8 children are coming to our party. If we share them fairly, how many balloons will each one receive?), and quotative division (e.g., Each child who comes to our party will receive 3 balloons. We have 24 balloons. How many children can we invite?) (see Fischbein et al. 1985).
   When the unit ratio is not given (e.g., If you shell 12 kilos of shrimp, you get 8 kilos of shelled shrimp. If you want 12 kilos of shelled shrimp, how many kilos of shrimp do you have to catch?), the problems are termed proportions problems.
2. Situations that involve an inverse relation between two quantities, including intensive quantities: For example, problems that involve density of objects in a space in which the total space is directly proportional to the density and the number of objects is inversely proportional to the density; problems about speed in which the time is inversely proportional to the speed and the distance covered is directly proportional to the speed; and problems that involve cost in which the amount purchased is inversely proportional to the cost and the price paid is directly proportional to the cost (Howe et al. 2010, 2011; Nunes et al. 2003; Schwartz 1988).
3. Situations in which a third quantity is formed by two quantities: For example, using two types of bread and four fillings, one can form eight different sandwiches and using four skirts and five tops, one can wear 20 different outfits. These problems have been termed Cartesian or product of measures problems (Brown 1981a, b; Vergnaud 1983).
4. Multiple proportions situations, in which one quantity is proportionally related to more than one other quantity: for example, a farmer's milk production is related to the number of cows, the productivity of each cow per day, and the number of days (Vergnaud 1983).

Multiplicative reasoning has been analyzed in a huge number of studies. Some of the well-established conclusions are summarized here.

First, when the unit value is given and manipulable representations are provided for children to construct a representation of the relations between quantities, the level of success of 5- and 6-year-olds has been surprisingly high: about two thirds succeeded in multiplication and partitive division problems and more than one third in quotative division (Nunes et al. 2008). Multiplication and partitive division have similar levels of difficulty; quotative division problems are more difficult (Bell et al. 1984; Correa et al. 1998; for a review, see Greer 1992). Problems are more difficult when the unit value is not given; when the unknown value is larger than the known, non-unitary value, problems are easier than when the unknown is smaller (Nunes et al. 1993, 2003).

Second, problems are generally easier if the proportional relation is direct rather than inverse. However, problems that involve speed tend not to follow this generalization (Howe et al. 2010; Nunes and Bryant 2008; Nunes et al. 2003).

Third, many students seem to hold several misconceptions about multiplication and division: for example, that multiplication makes bigger and division makes smaller and that you cannot divide a smaller number by a bigger number (Bell et al. 1981, 1984; De Corte et al. 1988). It has been noted that these misconception were also identified in prospective primary school teachers in the United States: 24 % of the teachers interviewed about multiplication and division problems in which they had used the inappropriate operation expressed some form of belief that multiplication makes numbers bigger and division makes numbers smaller (Graeber et al. 1989). These researchers also found that prospective teachers made inappropriate analogies between ways of solving problems. For example, in the problem, "From 1 kg of wheat you get 0.75 kg of flour. How much flour do you get from 15 kg of wheat?" they argued that "they were looking for part of a quantity. And since one finds 1/2 of 6 by dividing 6 by 2, one also finds 0.75 of 15 by dividing 15 by 0.75" (Graeber et al. 1989, p. 98). We conjecture that these students and prospective teachers might have had more instruction on arithmetic than on quantitative reasoning.

Fourth, there are two invariants that can be used to solve proportions problems. Figure 3 illustrates a problem presented to fishermen in Brazil by Nunes et al. (1993). Fishermen learn the relations between quantities that are relevant to their work on the job. Most had not attended school beyond fourth grade; proportions are taught in sixth grade. The problem was: "When you shell 18 kg of shrimp, you end up with 3 kg of shelled shrimp. If a customer wanted 2 kg of shelled shrimp, how much would you have to catch?" Figure 3 presents schematically the two invariants in the problem: the functional and the scalar. The values were chosen not to be realistic, so that the fishermen would need to calculate the answer, and so that the functional solution would be easier to calculate than the scalar solution: dividing 18 by 3, which leads to identifying the functional invariant, is likely to be easier than dividing 3 by 2, which involves a fraction and leads to the identification of the scalar solution.

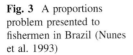
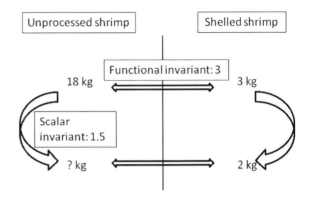

Fig. 3 A proportions problem presented to fishermen in Brazil (Nunes et al. 1993)

In spite of the relative ease of the functional solution, most fishermen preferred the scalar solution, which is clearly much more awkward in this example. Their calculation was not driven by the numbers but by reasoning. One fisherman's response is transcribed here to illustrate his solution.

> Fisherman: One and a half kilos [shelled] would be nine [unprocessed]; *it has to be nine because half of eighteen is nine and half of three is one and a half.* And a half-kilo [processed] is three kilos [unprocessed]. Then it'd be nine plus three is twelve [unprocessed]; the twelve kilos would give you the two kilos [processed] (Nunes et al. 1993, p. 112).

The preference for scalar over functional reasoning has been well documented in the literature in different countries; teaching algorithms for solving proportions problems (such as the Rule of Three) seems to have a relatively limited impact on students' approaches to solution (Hart 1981; Noelting 1980a, b; Vergnaud 1983).

Fifth, errors in proportions problems are extremely common even after instruction (e.g., Lesh et al. 1988; Singer et al. 1997). Many errors involve using additive reasoning instead of multiplicative reasoning. Inhelder and Piaget (1958) suggested that, when children first start to reason about relations, they do so by using additive reasoning, and only in a later stage of development they become able to use multiplicative reasoning. However, errors in additive problems can sometimes be due to the overuse of multiplicative reasoning, both among students (De Bock et al. 2002) and prospective teachers (Cramer et al. 1993). Nunes and Bryant (2015) have thus urged for studies that investigate this question more systematically.

In summary, research on the development of additive and of multiplicative reasoning reveals that students can demonstrate difficulties in problem solving even after instruction. This has also been documented with prospective teachers. Once again, the unavoidable conclusion is that the teaching of quantitative reasoning must become a theme in mathematics education curricula.

2.5   Teaching Quantitative Reasoning

Word problems are texts that typically contain quantitative information. They typically "describe a situation assumed familiar to the reader and pose a quantitative question, an answer to which can be derived by mathematical operations performed on the data provided in the text, or otherwise inferred" (Greer et al. 2002, p. 271). Most curricula contain word problems; associations of teachers of mathematics (e.g., NCTM 1989, 1999, 2000) recommend their use in teaching as a means of helping students to connect mathematics with the world outside the classroom. The literature has seen much controversy about the value of word problems, which will not be reviewed here due to space limitations. Suffice it to say that the criticism has often not been about the use of language in the classroom to present situations in which mathematical reasoning is relevant, but to the ways in which word problems have been used in the classroom. Word problems in primary school have been used often (with notable exceptions, exemplified by the work of researchers at the Freudenthal Institute) as the application of arithmetic procedures that have just been taught. When used in this way, the practice brings with it implicit assumptions that seem to restrict students' reasoning and even their willingness to reason (see, for example, Chapman 2006; Chevallard 1988; Greer et al. 2002; and the excellent review by Verschaffel et al. 2010). We review in this section three different approaches to teaching quantitative reasoning, all of which use word problems as a starting point: (1) teaching quantitative reasoning before teaching arithmetic, (2) schema-based instruction, and (3) using pre-designed diagrams.

2.5.1   Teaching Quantitative Reasoning Before Arithmetic

Researchers at the Freudenthal Institute have typically used word problems to create situations that students can mathematize; in this process, they develop an understanding of arithmetic. Freudenthal wrote:

> I espouse the philosophy of teaching mathematics related to reality. Mathematics is important for many people because it admits of multifarious applications. I do not trust teachers of other disciplines to be able to tie the bonds of mathematics with reality which have been cut by the mathematics teacher. Moreover, I do not believe that mathematics, not tied to lived reality with strong bonds, can have a lasting influence in most individuals (Freudenthal 1971, p. 420).

The consequence of the idea of teaching mathematics related to reality is that, in the approach developed at the Freudenthal Institute, learning about numbers and arithmetic starts from situations which students are invited to mathematize rather than the other way around (i.e., rather than learning first arithmetic and then attempting to connect it to reality through application in word problems). Teaching about natural numbers takes place through the solution of addition and subtraction problems as the basis for understanding natural numbers and learning about computation (Van den Brink 1991); solving problems that involve ratio (e.g., 6 parents can sit at a table and 81 parents are coming to the school: How many tables do we need?) is the starting point for learning how to calculate multiplication and division (Gravemeijer 1997; Treffers 1991) and for understanding fractions (Streefland 1991, 1997). Geometry teaching also starts from activities that involve reasoning about space (De Moor 1991; Van Hiele 1999) and perspective (Van den Brink and Streefland 1979) before formalization.

Studies in which teaching starts from analyzing relations between quantities often focus on a single but broadly defined concept—for example, proportions (Kaput and West 1994), fractions (Olive and Steffe 2002; Nunes et al. 2007), speed (Thompson 1994), or rate of change (Confrey 1994). These studies are similar in purpose and spirit to the studies carried out at the Freudenthal Institute because they all focus on quantitative reasoning rather than arithmetic in problem solving. Following Piaget (1950), these different mathematics education researchers proposed that children form schemes of action that help them understand situations (e.g., Cobb and Von Glasersfeld 1983; Nunes and Bryant 1996; Steffe 1994; Steffe and Thompson 2000; Vergnaud 2009; Von Glasersfeld 1981); these schemes are the focus of instruction.

In the approach used at the Freudenthal Institute, students are encouraged to use simpler mathematical representation tools that are closer to their own thinking before they are taught about formalizations. Space does not permit a review of the huge number of papers which describe the ingenuity of teaching mathematics in this way. We present one example about teaching proportional reasoning.

Streefland (1984, 1985) proposed that an effective way to help students to master proportional reasoning was to offer them a representational tool, which he called the ratio table, that they could use to represent their own reasoning. Research (see previous section) had established that students have a firm grasp of scalar reasoning; this ratio reasoning can be represented initially with drawings and later on in the ratio table. Copyright issues do not allow us to include Streefland's own drawings; we include here those obtained in a study by Nunes and colleagues, which used his approach.

The students who participated in this study were in fifth grade (ages 10–11) in Oxford; they had not been taught about proportions in school. They were participating in a randomized controlled study that included three groups: one taught about quantitative reasoning in situations that involve certainty, one taught about probabilities, and one was an unseen control group. The inclusion of the group taught about probabilities aimed to assess transference of reasoning across rather different situations; the details cannot be discussed here (for details, see Nunes et al. 2015a).The children participated in 15 small group lessons, which were run by the researchers in order to facilitate observation and discussion of their problem-solving procedures. The ratio table was introduced in the eighth lesson; the previous lessons were about the inverse relation between operations and directed (positive and negative) numbers. Figure 4 (left) presents the problem used in this study, adapted from Van Den Brink and Streefland (1979). The children were told that Dazz and Mrs. Elastic were racing; when Mrs. Elastic took 6 steps, Dazz had to take 10 to keep up. They were presented with the diagram on a white board and asked to fill in

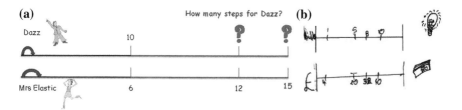

Fig. 4 **a** The problem used to introduce the ratio table. **b** A child's ratio table for a different problem

the information: When Mrs. Elastic took 12 steps, how many would Dazz take? When Mrs. Elastic took 15 steps, how many would Dazz take? The numbers were chosen so that scalar reasoning was easily used; 12 is twice 6, and 15 is 12 plus half of 6. The children found the ratio diagram easy to use and were quick in applying it to other problems. A problem presented later on was: Paul replaced 5 energy saving bulbs in the bathroom and saved £20 that year. He then decided to replace all the bulbs in the kitchen as well. There are 8 bulbs in the kitchen. How much money will he save? This problem is not easily solved by doubling; it requires extending the scalar reasoning to the search for the unitary value. Figure 4b presents one student's solution.

A major advantage of the ratio table was that students did learn to organize their thinking, separating out the numbers that referred to each of the quantities. Whereas at the start they might have carried out computations without thinking about the quantities that the numbers represented, by using the diagram this was not a problem later on.

In two studies in which we used Streefland's ratio table, one in which the researchers taught small groups of children and another in which teachers used the program with their classes, we obtained positive results. Statistical analyses showed that the group that worked on quantitative reasoning made more progress in problem solving than the group that did not (Nunes et al. 2015a); however, this outcome cannot be attributed only to the use of the ratio table because the program involved other components.

In a recent study, Nunes et al. (2016) demonstrated the impact of teaching quantitative reasoning on children's mathematical achievement. In a large-scale randomized controlled trial, second graders who participated in a mathematical reasoning program that included no teaching of arithmetic performed significantly better than the children in the control group, both in problem solving and arithmetic. As the children did not have any extra time on mathematics teaching during this period, it seems safe to conclude that the improvements were an outcome of the teaching of quantitative reasoning.

Thus there is some evidence that children can benefit from teaching that focuses on quantitative reasoning and uses representational tools that help them mathematize situations.

2.5.2   Schema-Based Instruction

Schema-based instruction in problem solving has many proponents (e.g., Chen 1999; Fuchs et al. 2004a, b; Jitendra and Hoff 1996; Marshall 1995). The core idea behind schema-based instruction is that children can learn to classify problems into problem types, and then use the heuristic "what do I know that is similar to this problem" to design a path to solution. Prototypical problems that define the schema are presented in initial lessons and the paths to solution are exemplified and then modeled by the students; the hypothesis is that they will later identify analogous problems and use similar pathways to solution. To illustrate this approach, we describe the classification used in one study. Problems were drawn from the students' textbooks and classified under evocative names: for example:

> *Shopping list* (e.g., "Joe needs supplies for the science project. He needs 2 batteries, 3 wires, and 1 board. Batteries cost $4 each, wires cost $2 each, and boards cost $6 each. How much money does he need to buy supplies?"), *half* (e.g., "Marcy will buy 14 baseball cards. She'll give her brother half the cards. How many cards will Marcy have?"), *buying bags* (e.g., "Jose needs 32 party hats for his party. Party hats come in bags of 4. How many bags of party hats does Jose need?"), and *pictograph* (e.g., "Mary keeps track of the number of chores she does on this chart [pictograph is shown with label: each picture stands for 3 chores]. She also took her grandmother to the market 3 times last week. How many chores has Mary done?"). (Fuchs et al. p. 637)

Schema-based instruction often involves interaction between children during the discussion of which schema best fits with a problem; however, it has been found to improve children's problem-solving skills beyond the effects of peer interaction and to enhance problem-solving skills in children who have difficulties with mathematics (e.g., Fuchs et al. 2004a, b, 2010; Jitendra et al. 2007, 2009, 2011).

Although there is convincing evidence that schema-based instruction is effective, we note that the schemas proposed for the classification of problems are usually based on ad hoc classifications. It is puzzling that the researchers have not relied on the classification of additive and multiplicative reasoning problems found to describe levels of difficulty in mathematics education research and why they have often included surface features of problems in their classification schemas.

2.5.3   Instruction Based on Pre-designed Diagrams

Different definitions of diagrams have been proposed in the literature (e.g., Larkin and Simon 1987; Novick 2006; Novick and Hurley 2001), but all the definitions share the notion that diagrams are structural or functional analogs of what they represent. This characteristic is assumed to make diagrams good tools for thinking because "they simplify complex situations, make abstract concepts more concrete, and substitute easier perceptual inferences for more computationally intensive search processes and sentential deductive inferences" (Novick and Hurley 2001, p. 159). Diagrams are iconic models of situations; this allows them to represent explicitly topographical and geometric information about relations, which are often not represented in sentences (Dufour-Janvier et al. 1987; Larkin and Simon 1987; Johnson-Laird 1983). Different institutions that set goals and standards for mathematics teaching, such as the Australian Association of Mathematics Teachers (1997), the U.K. Department for Education and Employment (1998), and the U.S. National Council of Teachers of Mathematics (2000), have argued for the use of diagrams in mathematics education.

Researchers in mathematics education have hypothesized that diagrams fulfill at least two functions in mathematics learning. First, Murata and Fuson (Murata 2008; Murata and Fuson 2006) suggest that external visual representations can support communication between the teacher and the students, allowing the teacher to help students progress in the zone of proximal development; students will later be able to solve problems with the support of the diagrams and independently from the teacher. Second, Streefland (1987) and Gravemeijer (1997) suggest that diagrams can be mediators of the step from a concrete situation to a more abstract concept: a model *of* a situation can become a model *for* several situations. Gravemeijer (1997) further argued that diagrams designed without considering how students reason might not function very well in the process of horizontal mathematization, which aims to help students mathematize their own thinking.

A diagram that has attracted considerable interest in the study of problem solving is the Singapore Model Method (Ng and Lee 2009), which Murata (2008) sees as the same as the Tape Diagram used in Japan. In these diagrams, bars represent quantities and arrows represent relations between quantities. Complex problems that include many quantities and relations are expected to become accessible to students in fifth and sixth grade through the use of bar diagrams. For copyright reasons, we use here problems and diagrams from the study by Nunes et al. (2015a), which included the bar diagram as well as the ratio table. A complex problem used was: "Grade 4, Grade 5, and Grade 6 students played some games in a competition. The fourth graders won 3 more prizes than the fifth graders, and the sixth graders won 5 more prizes than the fourth graders. Altogether the three grade levels received 68 prizes. How many prizes did each grade level collect?" Figure 5a, left, presents a diagram for this problem; on the right, a student's production is presented (Figure 5b).

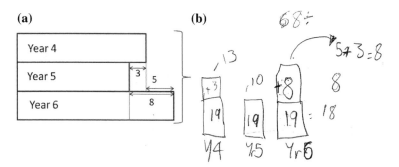

Fig. 5 a A diagram for a problem with many quantities and relations. **b** A student's diagram for this problem

The comparison between the two diagrams illustrates a common difference between the expected and the observed diagrams in this problem. Students often approached the problem by first guessing what the number of prizes might be if the three grade levels had the same number and then adjusted the solution by thinking about the differences. This student first guessed 20 for each class, tried to adjust for the differences and found that the total would go over 68. The student then guessed 18, found that the total would be less than 68, and then guessed 19, making the total number now correct. This was a particularly difficult problem because it involved the composition of relations: the difference between Grade 6 and Grade 5 has to be obtained by adding the difference between Grade 4 and Grade 5 and the difference between Grade 6 and Grade 4. The diagram in Fig. 5a, left, shows this composition of relations. The diagram did work as a tool for the student's reasoning and also for communication between the teacher and the students during the discussion that followed problem solution. However, most students persisted in starting with an educated guess about the amounts and adjusting for the differences afterwards rather than operating on the relations first and dividing later. The idealized diagram may have been too far from the students' own reasoning in this type of problem.

Nunes et al. (2015a) found a significant difference between the problem-solving group that used diagrams and the comparison groups but, as mentioned earlier on, this difference cannot be attributed to the use of the bar diagram, because this was only one of the parts of the teaching program.

In another study, Nunes et al. (2015b) assigned children randomly to one of four groups: two groups received instruction in problem solving with the support of diagrams (the bar diagram oran arrow diagram, previously used by Willis and Fuson (1988; Fuson and Willis 1989) and one received instruction without diagrams; the fourth group was an unseen control group. The three taught groups outperformed the unseen control group in a post-test, but there were no differences between the three taught groups; the group that solved the same problems without diagrams was as successful as the groups that used diagrams. Thus there was no evidence for a specific effect of diagram use. Nevertheless, the authors point out that the results might have been different if the intervention had been longer.

Studies using a broader definition of diagram, which includes drawings, have also investigated systematically its impact on problem solving. In two studies, Dewolf et al. (2014) presented 10- to 11-year-old children with word problems that were accompanied either by an illustration that depicted the situation or by a warning stating that some questions were nonstandard. Neither the illustrations nor the warning, nor even the combination of both, had a positive impact on the number of realistic solutions, which was the outcome measure. The authors were cautious about the interpretation of the results and conjectured that students may not have looked at the pictures or perhaps the pictures did not activate their real-world knowledge during problem solving.

In contrast to the study by Dewolf et al. (2014), in which the drawings were presented by the researchers, Csíkos et al. (2012) carried out a study in which the children generated their own illustrations. No effect of the use of drawings was found, even though their intervention was extensive and covered solving 73 problems over 20 lessons.

These recent studies converge with the conclusions put forth by Van Meter and Garner (2005) in a systematic review of the literature: the promise of improved learning with the use of drawings and diagrams has not been fulfilled. It is rather puzzling that the bar diagrams used in Singapore have attracted such praise (e.g., England 2010), but benefits of their use are yet to be demonstrated through systematic research.

3 Knowledge of Numbers and Arithmetic for Teaching

Knowing the subject well is fundamental for the job of teaching, but it is important to know what type of knowledge within the subject is significant for teaching and how it is measured. It is also important to know whether knowledge of the subject is sufficient for teaching. Dewey made a distinction between the knowledge required by the scientist for doing science and the knowledge required by the teacher and suggested that these two aspects are not opposed but neither are they identical (Dewey 1899/1990).

The awareness that teachers must know more than the subject in order to teach has been reflected in many publications in mathematics education since the 1970s. Some of the themes that are likely to have contributed to this awareness are identified here. Lovell (1972) suggested that the new way of thinking about teaching mathematics as the study of structures and patterns of relations promoted by the Bourbaki group of mathematicians prompted mathematics education researchers to look at the work of Piaget for directions on how to teach mathematics. Piaget's ideas about knowledge developing from interactions with the world were translated by many mathematics educators into the need to use manipulatives in teaching. It was apparent, then, that knowledge of the decimal structure of the number system and place value was not sufficient for teaching: teachers needed to have at their disposal objects that represented this structure in some way so that children could use analogies from physical objects to symbols. Kieren (1971) identified research questions that had to be addressed for the best possible use of manipulatives in the classroom.

Piaget's (1953) claim that children do not learn mathematical concepts just from teaching, as this learning also depends on the children's cognitive development, led to discussions on the distinction between expository and discovery methods in mathematics learning (e.g., Olander and Robertson 1973), which became another theme of investigation in mathematics education. This theme then led to the study of teachers' attitudes towards mathematics: do teachers see mathematics as a set of ready-made concepts or as an activity (e.g., Collier 1972)? The latter theme appears to have become less influential in research in the last 20 years, but many papers were published previously on teachers' attitudes towards mathematics.

Another theme in research that suggests an awareness that teachers' knowledge is different from subject knowledge is the recognition that appropriate mathematical descriptions can lead to different algorithms: teachers need to decide which algorithm should be taught (see, for example, research about which is the best division algorithm to teach and how to teach it in Kratzer and Willoughby 1973).

Finally, mathematics education researchers recognized early on that general descriptions of teachers' behaviors and general pedagogical knowledge do not offer mathematics teachers sufficient guidance for teaching mathematics: teachers must know specific ways of teaching students about specific concepts (e.g., Flora 1972; Cooney and Henderson 1972).

However, it is since Shulman's (1986) now classic paper that the distinction between content knowledge and pedagogical content knowledge became a central theme in research on teacher education. Content knowledge defines an expert: Shulman asked how does an expert mathematician, for example, become a novice mathematics teacher? Shulman anticipated what constitutes the core of pedagogical content knowledge when he proposed a research program about this domain:

> Within the category of pedagogical content knowledge I include … the most useful forms of representation of those ideas, the most powerful analogies, illustrations, examples, explanations, and demonstrations—in a word, the ways of representing and formulating the subject that make it comprehensible to others. … Pedagogical content knowledge also includes an understanding of what makes the learning of specific topics easy or difficult: the conceptions and preconceptions that students of different ages and backgrounds bring with them. (Shulman 1986, p. 9)

Shulman's statement is not neutral with respect to the aims of education: given that the aim of teaching is to make the subject comprehensible to others, it does not align with the traditional teaching to which the New Math and the constructivist movements objected. His ideas took form in an educational context in which the search for meaningful learning and the fact that children's own thinking might make some topics difficult were assumptions taken for granted.

In a survey carried out on behalf of ICME, Adler et al. (2005) considered the creation of the *Journal of Mathematics Teacher Education* in 1998 an indication of the growing significance of teachers' knowledge as a research theme. The task for researchers in mathematics education in the last 25 years since the inception of the journal has been to identify ways of conceiving and measuring content knowledge and pedagogical content knowledge. The number of mathematics courses taken during teacher education does not predict students' achievement, according to a review by the National Mathematics Advisory Panel (2008). However, this finding did not lead the Panel to conclude that content knowledge is irrelevant to teaching mathematics. In fact, the Panel saw number of courses taken only as a proxy for measuring content knowledge; their conclusion was that the results of the studies were mixed but overall did confirm the importance of teachers' content knowledge.

3.1 Describing Teachers' Content Knowledge and Its Impact

The literature on primary school teachers' content knowledge (including prospective teachers) is vast and cannot be reviewed here in detail (for a review and critique, see Mewborn 2001). We use here as an example the work of Tchoshanov (2011), who attempted a classification of the types of knowledge required for teaching mathematics (for a different approach, see Ball, Thames and Phelps 2008). Three types of knowledge were distinguished:

Type 1: Knowledge of Facts and Procedures. This kind of knowledge reflects memorization of facts, definitions, formulas, properties, and rules; performing procedures and computations; making observations; conducting measurements; and solving routine problems.

Type 2: Knowledge of Concepts and Connections. This type includes, but is not limited to the following: understanding concepts, making connections, selecting and using multiple representations, transferring knowledge to a new situation, and solving non-routine problems.

Type 3: Knowledge of Models and Generalizations. This type requires thinking for generalization of mathematical statements, designing mathematical models, making and testing conjectures, and proving theorems (Tchoshanov 2011, p. 148).

Working with a large sample of teachers, Tchoshanov (2011) found little variation in teachers' Type 1 and Type 3 knowledge, but considerable variation in Type 2. This meant that the correlations between Types 1 and 3 knowledge and student achievement could not be significant; in contrast, there was a significant correlation between student achievement and teachers' Type 2 knowledge. Tchoshanov's (2011) study represents a significant step in developing a conceptual measure of teachers' mathematics content knowledge and provides clear evidence of a connection between student achievement and teachers' content knowledge. We note that Type 2 knowledge is similar to Shulman's description of pedagogical content knowledge, but does not exhaust it.

3.2 Describing Teachers' Pedagogical Content Knowledge

Although there may be different interpretations of Shulman's ideas about content knowledge and pedagogical content knowledge, some researchers have found that these two are clearly related (e.g., Baumert et al. 2010; Hill 2010), particularly when the measures used focus on the same topic—for example, knowledge of operations with fractions and knowledge of ways of explaining operations with fractions. In some studies, content knowledge and pedagogical content knowledge appear to be less correlated because the measures address different topics (e.g., teachers' knowledge of probabilities and their pedagogical content knowledge about fractions). When statistical models have been used to analyze the strength of the connection between content knowledge, on the one hand, and pedagogical content knowledge, on the other hand, and students' learning, it has been found that pedagogical content knowledge is a mediator in the prediction; it explains extra variance in students' achievement beyond content knowledge, whereas content knowledge does not explain variance beyond pedagogical content knowledge (Baumert et al. 2010; Hill 2010). However, these results are difficult to interpret in view of the strong connection between the two. Baumert and colleagues suggest that content knowledge is necessary, but not sufficient, for promoting students' learning.

However, it is possible to classify measures as describing content or pedagogical content knowledge. Wheeler and Feghali's (1983) study on teachers' understanding of zero, for example, is classified by the authors themselves as a study of teachers' content knowledge, which seemed appropriate to us. Wheeler and Feghali asked prospective teachers to solve a few tasks that involved zero. Teachers had great difficulty in an arithmetic task that had a number different from zero as a dividend and zero as a divisor: 63 % of the participants answered incorrectly all six items of this type. When asked to explain their answers, few referred to multiplication (i.e., no number multiplied by zero can have a product different from zero), even among those who had given the correct answer. This failure to demonstrate an understanding of the inverse relation between division and multiplication clearly falls in the domain of knowledge of arithmetic—i.e., content knowledge.

Division and fraction arithmetic are considered by some the most difficult topics in primary school mathematics; consequently, teachers' knowledge of division and fractions has been investigated in many studies. Tirosh and colleagues (Even and Tirosh 1995, 2002; Tirosh 2000; Tirosh et al. 1998; Tirosh and Graeber 1989, 1990; Tsamir et al. 2000) have contributed substantially to this literature, along with many others (e.g., Ball 1990; Leinhardt and Smith 1985; Post et al. 1991; Quinn et al. 2008; Simon 1993; Simon and Schifter 1991). Some of the questions used in these studies focus on teachers' ability to solve tasks—i.e., content knowledge—whereas others focus on their ability to anticipate and explain students' errors—i.e., pedagogical content knowledge. To illustrate this research, we refer to Tirosh's study (2000) of prospective teachers' conceptions of division and fractions. Two of the arithmetic tasks presented to the teachers were: $1/4 \div 4$ and $320 \div 1/3$. The majority of participants (83 %) answered these items correctly; the errors observed were due to incorrect use of the division algorithm (e.g., $1/4 \div 4 = 1/4 \times 4 = 1$ or $320 \div 1/3 = 320/3 = 106.666$). One of the word problems presented was: a 5 m long stick is divided into 15 equal sticks; what is the length of each stick? (In all problems, the dividend was numerically smaller than the divisor.) All but one of the teachers (96.7 %) answered the problems correctly. The majority of the teachers (90 %) correctly anticipated at least one of the common errors that children make in the arithmetic tasks and most attributed the errors to faulty recollection of the algorithms. In contrast, only four (13.3 %) anticipated that the children might swap the dividend and the divisor in the problems due to the incorrect belief that dividends must be larger than divisors. These four teachers were aware of children's beliefs that multiplication makes bigger and division makes smaller and thought that these beliefs could lead to errors. The remaining teachers suggested that if the children had been well taught they would not make errors, or that their errors would result from reading comprehension or attention problems.

Tirosh's study included a teaching component, which focused both on content and pedagogical content knowledge. A typical comment by the prospective teachers was that they knew how to use the algorithms for calculating with fractions but did not know why they worked; thus the content knowledge element of the teaching intervention focused on understanding the algorithms. This allowed teachers to realize that faulty recollection of algorithms could be due to lack of understanding. The pedagogical content knowledge activities focused on devising explanations (for example, how do you explain to students why $2/3 \div 1/3 = 2$?) and extending the teachers' own understanding of division (most thought of division as sharing and did not think of measurement situations: i.e., how many times does x fit into y?) This extension of the teachers' understanding of division was both about content and pedagogical content knowledge: it was at the same time increasing the depth of their knowledge and providing them with situations that they could use in the classroom to promote thinking about division.

Content and pedagogical content knowledge also overlap when teachers attempt to understand why some concepts are difficult for students. Shulman referred to understanding the source of difficulty as knowing that some concepts require conceptual change; in the French literature, the same idea is described as an epistemological obstacle (Brousseau 1983). It is difficult to know, for example, whether teachers' realization that rational numbers do not have a next number is a matter of content or pedagogical content knowledge (Vamvakoussi and Vosniadou 2004): do teachers need to be more aware of this difference between whole and rational numbers themselves or do they need to realize that this is not obvious to their students in order to create tasks in which students encounter the challenge of not being able to say what the next number is?

A different approach to the study of pedagogical content knowledge is exemplified by the work of Carpenter, Fennema, and colleagues (Carpenter et al. 1989; Fennema et al. 1996). Their studies, known as cognitively guided instruction, do not focus on content knowledge, but exclusively on children's thinking: how to understand it and how to promote it. This is a significant tradition of research, which has strong implications for teacher education.

Lee and Lin (2016) conducted a systematic review of studies of teachers' knowledge between 2000 and 2015 to examine how pedagogical content knowledge has been investigated in this millennium. They reported the details of the process of identification and of categorization of papers. Here we report their main findings.

- The number of studies with teachers increased in the last five-year period.
- The majority of studies was with prospective rather than in-service teachers; this is probably due to teacher educators collecting data with their students in order to provide a basis for or to analyze their own practice (e.g., Isik and Kar 2012; Lo and Luo 2012; Newton 2008, 2009; Osana and Royea 2011).

- The topics most often studied were whole numbers, fractions, and properties of numbers and operations.
- When comparing content knowledge with pedagogical content knowledge, Lee and Lin (2016) concluded that researchers in mathematics education placed greater effort in exploring the degree of teachers' content knowledge of arithmetic than their pedagogical content knowledge.
- In these studies, written tests were the most frequently used method of data collection, followed by interviews/discussions and questionnaires; very few studies used teaching mathematical topics to teachers as the method for collecting data. Notable exceptions were the studies by Osana and Royea (2011) and by Toluk-Uçar (2009).

3.3   Other Perspectives on Teachers' Knowledge

Although much of the research on teachers' knowledge has focused on content and on pedagogical content knowledge, a review of teachers' knowledge could be considered remiss for not going outside this framework in order to mention that teachers also need to have an awareness of aspects of teaching that go beyond the particular tasks they propose to students. Chevallard's (1985) idea that a body of knowledge (such as mathematics) is constructed to be used, not to be taught, requires that teachers reflect beyond content knowledge to consider how a tool can be transformed into something to be taught and learned (see also Balacheff 1990). This didactical transposition, as Chevallard termed it, requires organizing mathematics for teaching differently from mathematics. This task is not entirely under the control of the teacher, as it is also influenced by the curriculum and by society. Why, when, and how concepts become part of the curriculum define mathematics for teaching; teachers enact this transposition. Content knowledge and pedagogical content knowledge take the didactical transposition for granted. Didactical transposition is a highly relevant idea when it comes to the themes investigated in mathematics education research: the large number of studies in the 1980s and 1990s that investigated ways of teaching the written calculation algorithms take for granted that these should be taught. Research on the use of calculators and spreadsheets also reflects the organization of mathematics as something to be taught; the tools for calculation become objects for teaching and learning.

A second construct that does not fit into the content and pedagogical content knowledge description is Brousseau's (1984, 1997) conception of the didactical contract. It refers to implicit aspects of what takes place in the classroom; some of these may actually result in obstacles to learning, known as pedagogical obstacles. Research with teachers and children as well has revealed interesting aspects of learners' conceptions that relate to the didactical contract. We exemplify by reference to division, which was discussed in the previous section: if the dividend is always bigger than the divisor in tasks used to introduce the concept of division, learners assume that this must always be the case. In problems that require division, if the divisor is bigger than the dividend, learners often swap the dividend and the divisor (see, for example, Greer 1988; Graeber et al. 1989). Schoenfeld (1988) noted that a major obstacle to problem solving among adults was the belief that, if you understand the concept involved in a mathematical problem, most problems can be solved in five minutes or less. This belief was presumably learned as part of the didactical contract in the classrooms attended by these adults (see also Nesher 1980).

At the close of this discussion, we suggest that the time may be ripe for wider theories that integrate the concepts of didactical transposition and didactical contract into the description of teachers' knowledge for teaching. Hiebert and Grouws (2007) as well as Oonk et al. (2015) argue for the need of a theory of reflective practice, which enriches practice with theoretical knowledge.

In summary, the idea that knowledge for doing science and knowledge for teaching science are different is more than a century old, but the systematic investigation of content and pedagogical content knowledge in mathematics education research is only about a half century old. Although these forms of knowledge are difficult to assess, and indeed difficult to disentangle from one another, much progress has been made in the domain of understanding what is needed for teaching mathematics in primary school. Research on teachers' thinking has made significant contributions to the development of teacher education (Clark and Lampert 1986; Lampert 1988; Lampert and Graziani 2009) and has the potential to support policy development in the future.

4 Summary and Challenges for the Future

In this summary, we attempt to bring together the different ideas presented throughout this review, rather than list them in succession, and outline some of the challenges for the future.

1. The context for the development of mathematics education research from the 1970s onwards was defined by influences from both inside and outside mathematics education. The New Math movement represented the questioning of teaching of rules without meaning. However, New Math did not succeed in the process of didactical transposition: mathematicians, scientists, and society as well did not identify New Math as the mathematics that they thought was useful and should be taught. At the same time, Piaget's constructivism was raising questions about the teaching of mathematics without understanding. Studies of children's cognitive development led to querying what and when children could be taught sensibly about numbers and other mathematical concepts (length, area, proportions, etc.). Much research in mathematics education in the 1970s focused on Piagetian concepts. Since then, the quest for meaning in mathematics education became well established in the research literature. This seems a major accomplishment in research; the challenge is to keep the search for meaning alive in the design of tasks and curricula.

2. An analysis of how numbers are used in mathematics reveals that numbers have two types of meaning: an analytical meaning, defined by the number system, and an extrinsic, representational meaning, in which numbers are signs for quantities or for relations between quantities. The analytical meaning defines arithmetic, which is the science of numbers and their behavior in the context of operations. The representational meaning is involved in quantitative reasoning, which refers to the understanding of relations between quantities (not relations between numbers) and their representation through numbers. The challenge for the future is to investigate more systematically the relation between these two types of number meaning. The psychological literature, not reviewed here for reasons of space, contains alternative hypotheses about this relation.

3. A traditional assumption in mathematics teaching has been that knowledge of arithmetic comes first; once arithmetic is learned, it becomes possible to apply it to quantitative reasoning. Much of the research in mathematics education in the 1980s and 1990s focused on how to teach arithmetic (written algorithms) in ways that would facilitate the understanding of relations between numbers. This research focused on the use of different types of manipulatives to represent the meaning of numbers in a place-value notation system and on the manipulations (such as exchange) that corresponded to the moves in column arithmetic. Subsequent research on arithmetic in the last 20 years focuses on mental arithmetic: researchers seek to understand and promote flexible thinking in solving computations. The challenge identified here is that there are different definitions of flexibility that lead to the use of different research methods and to different approaches to teaching. The search for a unifying definition could lead to fruitful collaboration across disciplines.

4. Researchers from the Freudenthal Institute and associated groups did not share the assumption that arithmetic comes before quantitative reasoning. Their assumption is that numbers should be used to represent quantities, changes in quantities, and relations between quantities; numbers should be useful from the start. From this quantitative reasoning, students develop an understanding of arithmetic, which can later be formalized by learning written algorithms, if desirable. Research on informal mathematics, which is learned and used outside school, provided results that are in line with the idea that quantitative reasoning can be powerful in the absence of knowledge of traditional computation algorithms. This research started in the 1980s and is still influential in mathematics education. The challenge for these researchers is that their view of mathematics for teaching does not match the didactical transposition process in many countries, where teaching arithmetic is seen as a primordial aim of mathematics education. Thus the internationalization of these ideas has been limited, in spite of their potential.

5. The 1980s and 1990s witnessed a surge of analyses of quantitative reasoning. Additive and multiplicative reasoning were analyzed by different groups, leading to converging results across countries about different types of problems and their levels of difficulty. The analysis of situations in which additive reasoning and multiplicative reasoning are used highlighted the significant difference between these two forms of reasoning—part-whole versus ratio—more than the overlaps between the two (division of a whole into parts allows for some overlap between

multiplication/division and part-whole reasoning; the distributive property of multiplication with respect to addition and of division with respect to subtractions allows for the use of addition and subtraction in calculating products and quotients). These studies underscore the significance of quantitative reasoning for arithmetic: young children understand subtraction, for example, only in relation to the act of taking away, but as they solve different types of problems they come to understand subtraction as the inverse of addition. The challenge for this research is to expand into ways of teaching that promote forms of reasoning that seem to remain elusive even after instruction (e.g., functional reasoning).

6. Research on how to promote quantitative reasoning has flourished since these developments. Different teaching approaches can be distinguished (starting from situations, using schemas for the classification of problems, using diagrams to represent quantities and relations between quantities). The challenge here is to carry out research that assesses these models in both short- and long-term studies and to avoid curriculum changes that implement models for teaching problem solving that have not been properly assessed.

7. Although researchers act as teachers in intervention studies, it seems inevitable that mathematics education research includes teachers both as learners and as teachers. The didactical transposition process means that mathematics for doing and mathematics for teaching are not the same thing; the conclusion is that teaching mathematics is necessary but not sufficient for learning how to teach mathematics. This idea is captured in research with teachers in the distinction between content and pedagogical content knowledge. These two forms of knowledge are related in practice and many teacher educators attempt to promote them together. If teachers only know, for example, the algorithms for computation with fractions and do not understand why they are different, they will not know how to explain them well; they are also likely to interpret children's errors as resulting from faulty recall, rather than lack of understanding. If teachers are not aware of the variety of situations in which an operation can be used—for example, division—they are likely to implement implicitly a didactical contract that restricts the meaning of division. It is arguable whether knowing a variety of situations to which division is relevant in order to promote a better understanding of the concept in the classroom is a matter of depth of content knowledge or a matter of pedagogical content knowledge. Even if this distinction is blurry at times, it is necessary in light of the process of didactical transposition, and has contributed to the strengthening of teacher education programs. The challenge is that mathematics education research is a moving target, and what we know today will not suffice tomorrow. Reflective practitioners, who are aware of research and enrich their practice by using theories, may develop in the future the wider teaching theories that some contend to be an achievable aim.

References

Adler, J., Ball, D., Krainer, K., Lin, F.-L., & Novotna, J. (2005). Reflections on an emerging field: Researching mathematics teacher education. *Educational Studies in Mathematics, 60*(3), 359–381.

Anghileri, J. (2001). Intuitive approaches, mental strategies and standard algorithms. In J. Anghileri (Ed.), *Principles and practices in arithmetic teaching: Innovative approaches for the primary classroom* (pp. 79–94). Suffolk: St. Edmundsbury Press.

Ashcroft, M. H., & Fierman, B. A. (1982). Mental addition in third, fourth and sixth graders. *Journal of Experimental Child Psychology, 33*, 216–234.

Australian Association of Mathematics Teachers. (1997). *Numeracy = everyone's business.* Australia: Adelaide.

Balacheff, N. (1990). Towards a problématique for research on mathematics teaching. *Journal for Research in Mathematics Education, 21*, 258–272.

Ball, D. L. (1990). Prospective elementary and secondary teachers' understanding of division. *Journal for Research in Mathematics Education, 21*(2), 132–144.

Ball, D. L., Thames, M. H., & Phelps, G. (2008). Content knowledge for teaching: What makes it special? *Journal of teacher education, 59*(5), 389–407.

Baroody, A. J. (1990). How and when should place-value concepts and skills be taught? *Journal for research in mathematics education, 21*(4), 281–286.

Baumert, J., Kunter, M., Blum, W., Brunner, M., Voss, T., Jordan, A., et al. (2010). Teachers' mathematical knowledge, cognitive activation in the classroom, and student progress. *American Educational Research Journal, 47*, 133–180.

Becher, R. M. (1978). The effects of perceptual transformation experiences and numerical operational experiences on numerical correspondence and equivalence. *Journal for Research in Mathematics Education, 9*(1), 69–74.

Becker, J. (1993). Young children's numerical use of number words: Counting in many-to-one situations. *Developmental Psychology, 19*, 458–465.

Beishuizen, M. (1993). Mental strategies and materials or models for addition and subtraction up to 100 in Dutch second grades. *Journal for Research in Mathematics Education*, 294–323.

Beishuizen, M., & Klein, A. S. (1998). The empty number line in Dutch second grades: Realistic versus gradual program design. *Journal for Research in Mathematics Education, 29*(4), 443–464.

Beishuizen, M., Van Putten, C. M., & Van Mulken, F. (1997). Mental arithmetic and strategy use with indirect number problems up to one hundred. *Learning and Instruction, 7*(1), 87–106.

Bell, A. W., Swan, M., & Taylor, G. (1981). Choice of operation in verbal problems with decimal numbers. *Educational Studies in Mathematics, 12*, 399–420.

Bell, A., Fischbein, E., & Greer, B. (1984). Choice of operation in verbal arithmetic problems: The effects of number size, problem structure and context. *Educational Studies in Mathematics, 15*, 129–147.

Bender, A., & Beller, S. (2011). Cultural variation in numeration systems and their mapping onto the mental number line. *Journal of Cross-Cultural Psychology, 42*, 579–597.

Blöte, A. W., Klein, A. S., & Beishuizen, M. (2000). Mental computation and conceptual understanding. *Learning and Instruction, 10*(3), 221–247.

Bobis, J. (2007). The empty number line: A useful tool or just another procedure? *Teaching Children Mathematics, 13*(8), 410–413.

Bramald, R. (2000). Introducing the empty number line. *Education, 3–13*(28), 5–12.

Brosseau, G. (1997). *Theory of didactical situations in mathematics*. Dordrecht, The Netherlands: Kluwer.

Brousseau, G. (1983). Les obstacles épistémologiques et les problèmes en mathématiques. *Recherches en Didactique des Mathématiques Grenoble, 4*(2).

Brousseau, G. (1984). The crucial role of the didactical contract in the analysis and construction of situations in teaching and learning mathematics. In H.-G. Steiner (Ed.), *Theory of mathematics education (TME) (ICME 5 -Topic Area and Miniconference: Adelaide, Australia)* (pp. 110–119). Bielefeld, Germany: Institut fur Didaktik der Mathematik, Universitat Bielefeld.

Brown, J. S., & Burton, R. R. (1978). Diagnostic models for procedural bugs in basic mathematical skills. *Cognitive Science, 2*(2), 155–192.

Brown, J. S., & VanLehn, K. (1982). Towards a generative theory of 'bugs'. In T. P. Carpenter, J. M. Moser, & T. A. Romberg (Eds.), *Addition and subtraction: A cognitive perspective* (pp. 117–135). Hillsdale, NJ: Erlbaum.

Brown, M. (1981a). Number operations. In K. Hart (Ed.), *Children's understanding of mathematics: 11–16* (pp. 23–47). Windsor, UK: NFER-Nelson.

Brown, M. (1981b). Place value and operations. In K. Hart (Ed.), *Children's understanding of mathematics: 11–16* (pp. 48–65). Windsor, UK: NFER-Nelson.

Bruner, J. S. (1966). *Toward a theory of instruction*. New York: Taylor & Francis.

Callahan, L. G., & Passi, S. L. (1971). The relationship between the ability to conserve length and conceptual tempo. *Journal for Research in Mathematics Education, 2*(1), 36–43.

Carpenter, T. P. (1975). Measurement concepts of first-and second-grade students. *Journal for Research in Mathematics Education, 6*(1), 3–13.

Carpenter, T. P., & Lewis, R. (1976). The development of the concept of a standard unit of measure in young children. *Journal for Research in Mathematics Education, 7*(1), 53–58.

Carpenter, T. P., & Moser, J. M. (1982). The development of addition and subtraction problem solving. In T. P. Carpenter, J. M. Moser, & T. A. Romberg (Eds.), *Addition and subtraction: A cognitive perspective* (pp. 10–24). Hillsdale (NJ): Lawrence Erlbaum.

Carpenter, T. P., Hiebert, J., & Moser, J. M. (1981). Problem structure and first grade children's initial solution processes for simple addition and subtraction problems. *Journal for Research in Mathematics Education, 12*, 27–39.

Carpenter, T. P., Matthews, W., Lindquist, M. M., & Silver, E. A. (1984). Achievement in mathematics: Results from the national assessment. *The Elementary School Journal, 84*(5), 484–495.

Carpenter, T. P., Fennema, E., Peterson, P. L., Chiang, C., & Loef, M. (1989). Using knowledge of children's mathematical thinking in classroom teaching: An experimental study. *American Educational Research Journal, 26*, 499–531.

Carpenter, T. P., Franke, M. L., Jacobs, V. R., Fennema, E., & Empson, S. B. (1997). A longitudinal study of invention and understanding in children's multidigit addition and subtraction. *Journal for Research in Mathematics Education, 29*, 3–20.

Carpenter, T. P., Franke, M. L., Jacobs, V. R., Fennema, E., & Empson, S. B. (1998). A longitudinal study of invention and understanding in children's multidigit addition and subtraction. *Journal for Research in Mathematics Education, 29*(1), 3–20.

Carroll, W. M. (1996). Use of invented algorithms by second graders in a reform mathematics curriculum. *The Journal of Mathematical Behavior, 15*(2), 137–150.

Cathcart, W. G. (1974). The correlation of selected nonmathematical measures with mathematics achievement. *Journal for Research in Mathematics Education, 5*(1), 47–56.

Chapman, O. (2006). Classroom practices for context of mathematics word problems. *Educational Studies in Mathematics, 62*(2), 211–230. doi: 10.1007/s10649-006-7834-1.

Chen, Z. (1999). Schema induction in children's analogical problem solving. *Journal of Educational Psychology, 91*, 703–715.

Chevallard, Y. (1985). *La transposition didactique (The didactical transposition)*. Grenoble, France: La Pensée Sauvage.

Chevallard, Y. (1988). The student-learner gap. In *Third Conference on the Theory of Mathematics Education, Anvers* (pp. 1–6), Text non publié. http://yves.chevallard.free.fr/spip/spip/IMG/pdf/On_Didactic_Transposition_Theory.pdf. Last accessed 25 April 2016.

Chung, M., & Bryant, P. (2001). The decimal system as a cultural tool: the case of additions and subtractions done by Korean and English children. *Korean Studies, 1*, 287–301.

Clark, C., & Lampert, M. (1986). The study of teacher thinking: Implications for teacher education. *Journal of Teacher Education, 37*(5), 27–31.

Cobb, P. (1987). Information processing psychology and mathematics education—A constructivist perspective. *The Journal of Mathematical Behavior, 6*, 4–40.

Cobb, P., & Von Glasersfeld, E. (1983). Piaget's scheme and constructivism: A review of misunderstandings. *Genetic Epistemology, 13*, 9–15.

Collier, C. P. (1972). Prospective elementary teachers' intensity and ambivalence of beliefs about mathematics and mathematics instruction. *Journal for Research in Mathematics Education, 3*(3), 155–163.

Confrey, J. (1994). Splitting, similarity and rate of change: A new approach to multiplication and exponential functions. In G. Harel & J. Confrey (Eds.), *The development of multiplicative reasoning in the learning of mathematics* (pp. 293–332). Albany, New York: State University of New York Press.

Cooney, T. J., & Henderson, K. B. (1972). Ways mathematics teachers help students organize knowledge. *Journal for Research in Mathematics Education, 3*(1), 21–31.

Correa, J., Nunes, T., & Bryant, P. (1998). Young children's understanding of division: The relationship between division terms in a noncomputational task. *Journal of Educational Psychology, 90*, 321–329.

Cramer, K., Post, T., & Currier, S. (1993). Learning and teaching ratio and proportion: Research implications. In D. T. Owens (Ed.), *Research ideas for the classroom: Middle grades mathematics* (pp. 159–178). New York: Macmillan.

Csíkos, C., Szitányi, J., & Kelemen, R. (2012). The effects of using drawings in developing young children's mathematical word problem solving: A design experiment with third-grade Hungarian students. *Educational Studies in Mathematics, 81*, 47–65.

De Bock, D., Van Dooren, W., Janssens, D., & Verschaffel, L. (2002). Improper use of linear reasoning: An in-depth study of the nature and the irresistibility of secondary school students' errors. *Educational Studies in Mathematics, 50*, 311–334.

De Corte, E., & Verschaffel, L. (1985). Beginning first graders' initial representation of arithmetic word problems. *Journal of Mathematical Behavior, 4*, 3–21.

De Corte, E., & Verschaffel, L. (1987). The effect of semantic structure on first graders' solution strategies of elementary addition and subtraction word problems. *Journal for Research in Mathematics Education, 18*, 363–381.

De Corte, E., Verschaffel, L., & Van Coillie, V. (1988). Influence of number size, problem structure and response mode on children's solutions of multiplication word problems. *Journal of Mathematical Behavior, 7*, 197–216.

De Moor, E. (1991). Geometry-instruction (age 4–14) in The Netherlands—The realistic approach. In L. Streefland (Ed.), *Realistic mathematics education in primary school* (pp. 119–138). Utrecht: Freudenthal Institute, Utrecht University.

Department for Education and Employment, UK. (1998). The implementation of the National Numeracy Strategy: The final report of the numeracy task force. London.

Dewey, J. (1899/1990). *The school and society: The child and the curriculum*. Chicago: University of Chicago.

Dewolf, T., Van Dooren, W., & Verschaffel, L. (2014). *The effect of visual aids in representational illustrations on realistic word problem solving*. Paper presented at the Special Interest Group 2, EARLI Conference, Rotterdam, The Netherlands. 25-27 August.

Dufour-Janvier, B., Bednarz, N., & Belanger, M. (1987). Pedagogical considerations concerning the problem of representation. In C. Janvier (Ed.), *Problems of representation in the teaching and learning of mathematics* (pp. 109–122). Hillsdale, NJ: Lawrence Erlbaum Associates.

England, L. (2010). Raise the bar on problem solving. *Teaching Children Mathematics, 17*, 156–163.

Even, R., & Tirosh, D. (1995). Subject-matter knowledge and knowledge about students as sources of teacher presentations of the subject-matter. *Educational Studies in Mathematics, 29*(1), 1–20.

Even, R., & Tirosh, D. (2002). Teacher knowledge and understanding of students' mathematical learning. *Handbook of international Research in Mathematics Education*, 219–240.

Fennema, E., Carpenter, T. P., Franke, M. L., Levi, L., Jacobs, V. R., & Empson, S. B. (1996). A longitudinal study of learning to use children's thinking in mathematics instruction. *Journal for Research in Mathematics Education, 27*, 403–434.

Fischbein, E., Deri, M., Nello, M., & Marino, M. (1985). The role of implicit models in solving verbal problems in multiplication and division. *Journal for Research in Mathematics Education, 16*, 3–17.

Flora, B. V. (1972). Diagnosing selected behavior characteristics of teachers of secondary school mathematics. *Journal for Research in Mathematics Education, 3*(1), 7–20.

Freudenthal, H. (1968). Why to teach mathematics so as to be useful. *Educational Studies in Mathematics, 1*(1/2), 3–8. Retrieved from http://www.jstor.org/stable/3481973

Freudenthal, H. (1971). Geometry between the Devil and the Deep Sea. *Educational Studies in Mathematics, 3*, 413–435.

Fuchs, L. S., Fuchs, D., Finelli, R., Courey, S. J., & Hamlett, C. L. (2004a). Expanding schema-based transfer instruction to help third graders solve real-life mathematical problems. *American Educational Research Journal, 41*, 419–445.

Fuchs, L. S., Fuchs, D., Prentice, K., Hamlett, C. L., Finelli, R., & Courey, S. J. (2004b). Enhancing mathematical problem solving among third grade students with schema-based instruction. *Journal of Educational Psychology, 96*, 635–647.

Fuchs, L. S., Zumeta, R. O., Schumacher, R. F., Powell, S. R., Seethaler, P. M., Hamlett, C. L., et al. (2010). The effects of schema-broadening instruction on second graders' word-problem performance and their ability to represent word problems with algebraic equations: A randomized control study. *The Elementary School Journal, 110*(4), 446.

Fuson, K. C., & Willis, G. B. (1989). Second graders' use of schematic drawings in solving addition and subtraction word problems. *Journal of Educational Psychology, 81*(4), 514–520.

Fuson, K. C. (1990a). Conceptual structures for multiunit numbers: Implications for learning and teaching multidigit addition, subtraction, and place value. *Cognition and Instruction, 7*(4), 343–403.

Fuson, K. C. (1990b). Issues in place-value and multidigit addition and subtraction learning and teaching. *Journal for Research in Mathematics Education, 21*(4), 273–280.

Fuson, K. C., & Briars, D. J. (1990). Base-ten blocks as a first-and second-grade learning/teaching approach for multidigit addition and subtraction and place-value concepts. *Journal for Research in Mathematics Education, 21*, 180–206.

Fuson, K. C., & Burghardt, B. H. (2013). Multidigit addition and subtraction methods invented in small groups and teacher support of problem solving and reflection. In A. J. Baroody & A. Dowker (Eds.), *The Development of Arithmetic Concepts and Skills: Constructive Adaptive Expertise* (pp. 267–307). London: Routledge.

Fuson, K. C., & Kwon, Y. (1992). Korean children's understanding of multidigit addition and subtraction. *Child Development, 63*, 491–506.

Fuson, K. C., Wearne, D., Hiebert, J. C., Murray, H. G., Human, P. G., Olivier, A. I., Carpenter, T., & Fennema, E. (1997). Children's conceptual structures for multidigit numbers and methods of multidigit addition and subtraction. *Journal for Research in Mathematics Education*, 130–162.

Gay, J., & Cole, M. (1967). *The New Mathematics and an Old Culture*. New York: Holt, Rhinehart and Winston.

Ginsburg, H. (1977). *Children's arithmetic*. New York: Van Norstrand.

Ginsburg, H. P. (1982). The development of addition in contexts of culture, social class, and race. In T. P. Carpenter, J. M. Moser, & T. A. Romberg (Eds.), *Addition and Subtraction: A cognitive Perspective* (pp. 191–210). Hillsdale, NJ: Lawrence Erlbaum.

Graeber, A. O., Tirosh, D., & Glover, R. (1989). Preservice teachers' misconceptions in solving verbal problems in multiplication and division. *Journal for Research in Mathematics Education, 20*, 95–102.

Gravemeijer, K., Heuvel, M. van den, & Streefland, L. (1990). Contexts free productions tests and geometry in realistic mathematics education. Utrecht: State University of Utrecht.

Gravemeijer, K. (1993). Modelling two-digit addition and subtraction with an empty number line. *Teaching and Learning Mathematics in Contexts*, 51–61.

Gravemeijer, K. (1997). Mediating between concrete and abstract. In T. Nunes & P. Bryant (Eds.), *Learning and Teaching Mathematics. An International Perspective* (pp. 315–346). Hove (UK): Psychology Press.

Greer, B. (1988). Nonconservation of multiplication and division: Analysis of a symptom. *Journal of Mathematical Behavior, 7*, 281–298.

Greer, B. (1992). Multiplication and division as models of situations. In D. Grouws (Ed.), *Handbook of research on mathematics teaching and learning* (pp. 276–295). New York: Macmillan.

Greer, B., Verschaffel, L, & De Corte, E. (2002). The answer is really 4.5: Beliefs about word problems. In G. C. Leder, E. Pehkonen & G. Törner (Eds.), *Beliefs: A hidden variable in mathematics education?* Dordrecht: Kluwer Academic Publishers.

Groen, G., & Resnick, L. (1977). Can pre-school children invent addition algorithms? *Journal of Educational Psychology, 69*, 645–652.

Grüßing, M., Schwabe, J., Heinze, A., & Lipowsky, F. (2013). The effects of two instructional approaches on 3rd-graders' adaptive strategy use for multi-digit addition and subtraction. In A. M. Lindmeier & A. Heinze (Eds.), *Proceedings of the 37th Conference of the International Group for the Psychology of Mathematics Education* (Vol. 2, pp. 393–401). Kiel: PME.

Guedj, D. (1998). *Numbers. A universal language*. London: Thame and Hudson.

Gullen, G. E. (1978). Set comparison tactics and strategies of children in kindergarten, first grade, and second grade. *Journal for Research in Mathematics Education, 9*(5), 349–360. http://doi.org/10.2307/748771

Hart, K. (1981). Ratio and proportion. In K. Hart (Ed.), *Children's understanding of mathematics: 11–16* (pp. 88–101). London: John Murray.

Hart, K., Brown, M., Kerslake, D., Küchermann, D., & Ruddock, R. (1985). *Chelsea diagnostic mathematics tests. Number concepts and operations*. Windsor (Berks): The NFER-NELSON Publishing Company Ltd.

Heinze, A., Marschick, F., & Lipowsky, F. (2009). Addition and subtraction of three-digit numbers: Adaptive strategy use and the influence of instruction in German third grade. *ZDM: The International Journal on Mathematics Education, 41*(5), 591–604.

Heirdsfield, A. M., & Cooper, T. J. (2002). Flexibility and inflexibility in accurate mental addition and subtraction: Two case studies. *Journal of Mathematical Behavior, 21*(1), 57–74.

Heirdsfield, A. M., & Cooper, T. J. (2004). Factors affecting the process of proficient mental addition and subtraction: Case studies of flexible and inflexible computers. *Journal of Mathematical Behavior, 23*(4), 443–463.

Hennessy, S. (1994). The stability of children's mathematical behavior: When is a bug really a bug? *Learning and Instruction, 3*(4), 315–338.

Hiebert, J., & Grouws, D. A. (2007). The effects of classroom mathematics teaching on students' learning. *Second Handbook of Research on Mathematics Teaching and Learning, 1*, 371–404.

Hiebert, J., & Wearne, D. (1996). Instruction, understanding, and skill in multidigit addition and subtraction. *Cognition and Instruction, 14*(3), 251–283.

Hill, H. C. (2010). The nature and predictors of elementary teachers' mathematical knowledge for teaching. *Journal for Research in Mathematics Education*, 513–545.

Ho, C. S. H., & Cheng, F. S. F. (1997). Training in place-value concepts improves children's addition skills. *Contemporary Educational Psychology, 22*(4), 495–506.

Hope, J. A. (1987). A case study of a highly skilled mental calculator. *Journal for Research in Mathematics Education, 18*(5), 331–342.

Howe, C., Nunes, T., Bryant, P., Bell, D., & Desli, D. (2010). Intensive quantities: Towards their recognition at primary school level *British Journal of Educational Psychology: Monograph Series II, Number 7: Understanding number development and difficulties*, 101–118.

Howe, C., Nunes, T., & Bryant, P. (2011). Rational number and proportional reasoning: Using intensive quantities to promote achievement in mathematics and science. *International Journal of Science and Mathematics Education, 9*, 391–417.

Hudson, T. (1983). Correspondences and numerical differences between sets. *Child Development, 54*, 84–90.

Huntington, J. R. (1970). Linear measurement in the primary grades: A comparison of piaget's description of the child's spontaneous conceptual development and the SMSG sequence of instruction. *Journal for Research in Mathematics Education, 1*(4), 219–232.

Inhelder, B., & Piaget, J. (1958). *The growth of logical thinking from childhood to adolescence.* New York: Basic books.

Isik, C., & Kar, T. (2012). An error analysis in division problems in fractions posed by pre-service elementary mathematics teachers. *Educational Sciences: Theory and Practice, 12*(3), 2303–2309.

Jitendra, A. K., & Hoff, K. (1996). The effects of schema-based instruction on mathematical word problem solving performance of students with learning disabilities. *Journal of Learning Disabilities, 29*, 422–431.

Jitendra, A. K., Griffin, C. C., Haria, P., Leh, J., Adams, A., & Kaduvettoor, A. (2007). A comparison of single and multiple strategy instruction on third-grade students' mathematical problem solving. *Journal of Educational Psychology, 99*, 115.

Jitendra, A. K., Star, J. R., Rodriguez, M., Lindell, M., & Someki, F. (2011). Improving students' proportional thinking using schema-based instruction. *Learning and Instruction, 21*(6), 731–745.

Jitendra, A. K., Star, J. R., Starosta, K., Leh, J. M., Sood, S., Caskie, G., … & Mack, T. R. (2009). Improving seventh grade students' learning of ratio and proportion: The role of schema-based instruction. *Contemporary Educational Psychology, 34*, 250–264.

Johnson, D. C. (1970). Editorial Comment. *Journal for Research in Mathematics Education, 1*(1), 5–6. Retrieved from http://www.jstor.org/stable/748916. Last accessed 25 April 2016.

Johnson-Laird, P. N. (1983). *Mental models.* Cambridge, MA: Harvard University Press.

Kaput, J. (1985). *Multiplicative word problems and intensive quantities: An integrated software response.* Cambridge (MA): Harvard University, Educational Technology Center.

Kaput, J., & West, M. M. (1994). Missing-value proprotional reasoning problems: Factors affecting informal reasoning patterns. In G. Harel & J. Confrey (Eds.), *The development of multiplicative reasoning in the learning of mathematics* (pp. 237–292). Albany, New York: State University of New York press.

Kidder, F. R. (1976). Elementary and middle school children's comprehension of Euclidean transformations. *Journal for Research in Mathematics Education, 7*(1), 40–52.

Kieren, T. E. (1971). Manipulative activity in mathematics learning. *Journal for Research in Mathematics Education, 2*(3), 228–234.

Klein, A. S., Beishuizen, M., & Treffers, A. (1998). The empty number line in Dutch second grades: Realistic versus gradual program design. *Journal for Research in Mathematics Education, 29*, 443–464.

Kratzer, R. O., & Willoughby, S. S. (1973). A comparison of initially teaching division employing the distributive and Greenwood algorithms with the aid of a manipulative material. *Journal for Research in Mathematics Education, 4*(4), 197–204.

Krauthausen, G. (1993). Kopfrechnen, halbschriftliches Rechnen, schriftliche Normalverfahren, Taschenrechner: Für eine Neubestimmung des Stellenwertes der vier Rechenmethoden [Mental arithmetic, informal strategies, written algorithms, calculators. A new role of routine procedures]. *Journal für Mathematik-Didaktik, 14*(3/4), 189–219.

Lampert, M. (1988). What can research on teacher education tell us about improving quality in mathematics education? *Teaching and Teacher Education, 4*(2), 157–170.

Lampert, M., & Graziani, F. (2009). Instructional activities as a tool for teachers' and teacher educators' learning. *The Elementary School Journal, 109*(5), 491–509.

Lancy, D. F. (1983). *Cross-cultural studies in cognition and mathematics*. New York: Academic Press.

Larkin, J. H., & Simon, H. A. (1987). Why a diagram is (sometimes) worth ten thousand words. *Cognitive Science, 11*, 65–99.

Lean, G. A. (1992). *Counting systems of Papua New Guinea and Oceania*. Papua New Guinea University of Technology.

Lee, H. F. & Lin, P. J. (2016). A review of number and arithmetic in teacher education. Paper will be presented at the 8th International Conference on Technology and Mathematics Education and Workshop of Mathematics Teaching (pp. 105–113). May 16–17, National Taichung University of Education, Taiwan.

Leinhardt, G., & Smith, D. (1985). Expertise in mathematics instruction: Subject matter knowledge. *Journal of Educational Psychology, 77*, 247–271.

Lesh, R., Post, T., & Behr, M. (1988). Proportional reasoning. In J. Hiebert & M. Behr (Eds.), *Number concepts and operations in the middle grades* (pp. 93–118). Reston, VA: National Council of Teachers of Mathematics.

Lester, F. K, Jr., & Steffe, L. P. (2013). Introduction/establishing mathematics education as an academic field: A constructive Odyssey. *Journal for Research in Mathematics Education, 44*(2), 353–371.

Lo, J. J., & Luo, F. J. (2012). Prospective elementary teachers' knowledge of fraction division. *Journal of Mathematics Teacher Education, 15*(6), 481–500.

Lovell, K. R. (1972). Intellectual growth and understanding mathematics. *Journal for Research in Mathematics Education, 3*(3), 164–182.

Mamede, E., Nunes, T., & Bryant, P. (2005). *The equivalence and ordering of fractions in part-whole and quotient situations*. Paper presented at the 29th Conference of the International Group for the Psychology of Mathematics Education, Melbourne.

Marshall, S. P. (1995). *Schemas in problem solving*. New York: Cambridge University Press.

Mewborn, D. (2001). Teachers content knowledge, teacher education, and their effects on the preparation of elementary teachers in the United States. *Mathematics Education Research Journal, 3*, 28–36.

Miller, K. F., & Stigler, J. W. (1987). Counting in Chinese: Cultural variation in a basic skill. *Cognitive Development, 2*, 279–305.

Miller, K. F., Smith, C. M., Zhu, J., & Zhang, H. (1995). Preschool origins of cross-national differences in mathematical competence: The role of number-naming systems. *Psychological Science, 6*, 56–60.

Miller, K. E., Smith, C. M., Zhu, J., & Zhang, H. (2000). Mathematical competence: The role of number-naming systems. In K. Lee (Ed.), *Childhood Cognitive Development: the essential readings* (pp. 123–154). Oxford: Blackwell.

Miura, I. T., Kim, C. C., Chang, & Okamoto, Y. (1988). Effects of language characteristics on children's cognitive representation of number: Cross-national comparisons. *Child Development, 59*, 1445–1450.

Miura, I. T., Okamoto, Y., Vlahovic-Stetic, V., Chungsoon, C. K., & Han, J. H. (1999). Language supports for children's understanding of numerical fractions: Cross-national comparisons. *Journal of Experimental Child Psychology, 74*, 356–365.

Moll, L. C., Mitchell, J., Simmons, W., & Scribner, S. (1984). Cognitive studies of work. *Laboratory of Comparative Human Cognition, 6*(1–2).

Mpiangu, B. D., & Gentile, J. R. (1975). Is conservation of number a necessary condition for mathematical understanding? *Journal for Research in Mathematics Education, 6*(3), 179–192.

Murata, A. (2008). Mathematics teaching and learning as a mediating process: The case of tape diagrams. *Mathematical Thinking and Learning, 10*, 374–406.

Murata, A., & Fuson, K. C. (2006). Teaching as assisting individual constructive paths within an interdependent class learning zone: Japanese first graders learning to add using ten. *Journal for Research in Mathematics Education, 37*, 421–456.

Murphy, C. (2011). Comparing the use of the empty number line in England and the Netherlands. *British Educational Research Journal, 37*(1), 147–161.

Murray, F. B. (1970). Verbal and nonverbal assessment of the conservation of illusion-distorted length. *Journal for Research in Mathematics Education, 1*(1), 9–18.

National Council of Teachers for Mathematics. (1989). *Curriculum and evaluation standards for school mathematics.* Reston, Virginia: NCTM.

National Council of Teachers of Mathematics. (1999). *Principles and standards for school mathematics.* Reston, Virginia: NCTM.

National Council of Teachers of Mathematics. (2000). *Principles and standards for school mathematics.* Reston, VA: NCTM.

National Mathematics Advisory Panel. (2008). *Foundations for success: The final report of the National Mathematics Advisory Panel.* Washington, DC: U.S. Department of Education.

Nesher, P. (1982). Levels of description in the analysis of addition and subtraction word problems. In T. P. Carpenter, J. M. Moser, & T. A. Romberg (Eds.), *Addition and subtraction.* Lawrence Erlbaum Ass: Hillsdale, NJ.

Nesher, P. (1980). The stereotyped nature of school word problems. *For the Learning of Mathematics, 1*, 41–48.

Newton, K. J. (2008). An extensive analysis of preservice elementary teachers' knowledge of fractions. *American Educational Research Journal, 45*(4), 1080–1110.

Newton, K. J. (2009). Instructional practices related to prospective elementary school teachers' motivation for fractions. *Journal of Mathematics Teacher Education, 12*, 89–109.

Ng, S. F., & Lee, K. (2009). The model method: Singapore children's tool for representing and solving algebraic word problems. *Journal for Research in Mathematics Education, 40*, 282–313.

Noelting, G. (1980a). The development of proportional reasoning and the ratio concept Part I— Differentiation of stages. *Educational Studies in Mathematics, 11*, 217–253.

Noelting, G. (1980b). The development of proportional reasoning and the ratio concept Part II— Problem-structure at sucessive stages: Problem-solving strategies and the mechanism of adaptative restructuring. *Educational Studies in Mathematics, 11*, 331–363.

Novick, L. R. (2006). Understanding spatial diagram structure: An analysis of hierarchies, matrices, and networks. *The Quarterly Journal of Experimental Psychology, 59*(10), 1826–1856.

Novick, L. R., & Hurley, S. M. (2001). To matrix, network, or hierarchy: That is the question. *Cognitive Psychology, 42*, 158–216.

Nunes Carraher, T., & Schliemann, A. D. (1985). Computation routines prescribed by schools: Help or hindrance? *Journal for Research in Mathematics Education, 16*(1), 37–44.

Nunes Carraher, T., Carraher, D. W., & Schliemann, A. D. (1985). Mathematics in the streets and in schools. *British Journal of Developmental Psychology, 3*, 21–29.

Nunes, T. (2002). The role of systems of signs in reasoning. In T. Brown & L. Smith (Eds.), *Reductionism and the development of knowledge* (pp. 133–158). Mawah (NJ): Lawrence Erlbaum.

Nunes, T., & Bryant, P. (1996). *Children doing mathematics.* Oxford: Blackwell.

Nunes, T., & Bryant, P. (2008). Rational numbers and intensive quantities: Challenges and insights to pupils' implicit knowledge. *Anales de Psicología, 24*(2), 262–270.

Nunes, T., & Bryant, P. (2015). The development of quantitative reasoning. In L. S. Liben & U. Müller (Eds.), *Handbook of child psychology and developmental science* (7 ed., Vol. 2. Cognitive Process, pp. 715–764). Hoboken, NJ: Wiley.

Nunes, T., Schliemann, A. D., & Carraher, D. W. (1993). *Street mathematics and school mathematics.* New York: Cambridge University Press.

Nunes, T., Desli, D., & Bell, D. (2003). The development of children's understanding of intensive quantities. *International Journal of Educational Research, 39*, 652–675.

Nunes, T., Bryant, P., Pretzlik, U., Bell, D., Evans, D., & Wade, J. (2007). La compréhension des fractions chez les enfants. In M. Merri (Ed.), *Activité humaine et conceptualisation* (pp. 255–262). Toulouse: Presses Universitaires du Mirail.

Nunes, T., Bryant, P., Burman, D., Bell, D., Evans, D., & Hallett, D. (2008). Deaf children's informal knowledge of multiplicative reasoning. *Journal of Deaf Studies and Deaf Education, 14*, 260–277.

Nunes, T., Bryant, P., Gottardis, L., Terlektsi, M.-E., & Evans, D. (2015a). Can we really teach problem solving in primary school? *Mathematics Teaching, 246*, 44–48.

Nunes, T., Leo, P., Shen, P., Evans, D., & Bryant, P. (2015b). *The use of diagrams to promote additive reasoning in primary school.* Paper presented at the EARLI Conference. Limassol (Cyprus), 24–30 August.

Nunes, T., Bryant, P., Evans, D., Barros, R., Chim, P., & Baker, S. (2016). *The significance of reasoning and arithmetic for mathematics achievement in primary school.* Paper presented at the International Conference in Mathematics Education (ICME), Hamburg, 24–31 July.

Olander, H. T., & Robertson, H. C. (1973). The effectiveness of discovery and expository methods in the teaching of fourth-grade mathematics. *Journal for Research in Mathematics Education, 4*(1), 33–44.

Olive, J., & Steffe, L. P. (2002). The construction of an iterative fractional scheme: The case of Joe. *Journal of Mathematical Behavior, 20*, 413–437.

Oonk, W., Verloop, N., & Gravemeijer, K. P. E. (2015). Enriching practical knowledge: Exploring student teachers' competence in integrating theory and practice of mathematics teaching. *Journal for Research in Mathematics Education, 46*(5), 559–598.

Osana, H. P., & Royea, D. A. (2011). Obstacles and challenges in preservice teachers' explorations with fractions: A view from a small-scale intervention study. *Journal of Mathematical Behavior, 30*, 333–352.

Owens, K. (2001). The work of Glendon Lean on the counting systems of Papua New Guinea and Oceania. *Mathematics Education Research Journal, 13*, 47–71.

Owens, D. T., & Steffe, L. P. (1972). Performance of kindergarten children on transitivity of three matching relations. *Journal for Research in Mathematics Education, 3*(3), 141–154.

Peters, D. L. (1970). Discovery learning in kindergarten mathematics. *Journal for Research in Mathematics Education, 1*(2), 76–87.

Piaget, J. (1950). *The psychology of intelligence.* London: Routledge.

Piaget, J. (1953). How children form mathematical concepts. *Scientific American, 189*(5), 74–79.

Poincaré, H. (2013/1908). *Science and méthod.* Paris: Courier Corporation. Retrieved from: http://henripoincarepapers.univ-lorraine.fr/chp/pdf/hp1999sm.pdf, last accessed 13 April 2016.

Post, T. R., Harel, G., Behr, M., & Lesh, R. (1991). Intermediate teachers' knowledge of rational number concepts. *Integrating research on teaching and learning mathematics*, 177–198.

Quinn, R. J., Lamberg, T. D., & Perrin, J. R. (2008). Teacher perceptions of division by zero. *The Clearing House: A Journal of Educational Strategies, Issues and Ideas, 81*(3), 101–104.

Rathgeb-Schnierer, E. (2006). *Kinder auf dem Weg zum flexiblen Rechnen: Eine Untersuchung zur Entwicklung von Rechenwegen von Grundschulkindern auf der Grundlage offener Lernangebote und eigenständiger Lösungsansätze* [Students develop flexibility in mental math: Study on development of calculation strategies based on an open approach]. Hildesheim; Berlin: Franzbecker.

Rathgeb-Schnierer, E. (2010). Entwicklung flexibler Rechenkompetenzen bei Grundschulkindern des 2. Schuljahrs [The development of flexible mental calculations of second graders]. *Journal für Mathematik-Didaktik, 31*(2), 257–283.

Rathgeb-Schnierer, E. (2011). Warum noch rechnen, wenn ich die Lösung sehen kann? Hintergründe zur Förderung flexibler Rechenkompetenzen [Why counting when I see the solution? Theoretical frameworks of teaching flexible mental calculation]. In R. Haug & L. Holzäpfel (Eds.), *Beiträge zum Mathematikunterricht* (pp. 15–22). Münster: WTM-Verlag.

Rechtsteiner-Merz, Ch. (2013). *Flexibles Rechnen und Zahlenblickschulung – eine Untersuchung zur Entwicklung von Rechenkompetenzen bei Erstklässlern, die Schwierigkeiten beim Rechnenlernen zeigen* [Flexible calculation and number sense—A study on numeracy skills of first graders with disabilities in learning mathematics]. Münster. Waxmann.

Rechtsteiner-Merz, Ch. & Rathgeb-Schnierer, E. (2015). Flexible mental calculation and "Zahlenblickschulung". In Krainer, K. & Vondrová, N. (Eds.), *Proceedings of the Ninth*

Congress of the European Society for Research in Mathematics Education (CERME9, 4–8 February 2015) (pp. 354–360). Prague, Czech Republic, Charles University in Prague, Faculty of Education and ERME.

Rathgeb-Schnierer, E. & Green, M. (2013). Flexibility in mental calculation in elementary students from different math classes. In Ubuz, B., Haser, Ç., & Mariotti, M. A. (Eds.), *Proceedings of the Eighth Congress of the European Society for Research in Mathematics Education* (pp. 353–362). Ankara: Middle East Technical University.

Reed, H. J., & Lave, J. (1981). Arithmetic as a tool for investigating relations between culture and cognition. In R. W. Casson (Ed.), *Language, culture and cognition: Anthropological perspectives* (pp. 437–455). New York: Macmillan.

Resnick, L. B. (1982). Syntax and semantics in learning to subtract. In T. P. Carpenter, J. M. Moser, & T. A. Romberg (Eds.), *Addition and subtraction: A cognitive perspective* (pp. 136–155). Hillsdale, NJ: Erlbaum.

Resnick, L. B. (1983). A developmental theory of number understanding. In H. P. Ginsburg (Ed.), *The development of mathematical thinking* (pp. 110–152). New York: Academic Press.

Riggs, F. T., & Nelson, L. D. (1976). Verbal-nonverbal conservation and primary mathematics. *Journal for Research in Mathematics Education, 7*(5), 315–320.

Romberg, T. A. (1982). An emerging paradigm for research on addition and subtraction skills. In T. P. Carpenter, J. M. Moser, & T. A. Romberg (Eds.), *Addition and subtraction: A cognitive perspective* (pp. 1–7). Hillsdale, NJ: Lawrence Erlbaum Associates Inc.

Romberg, T. A., & Gilbert, L. E. (1972). The effect of training on length on the performance of kindergarten children on nonstandard but related tasks. *Journal for Research in Mathematics Education, 3*(2), 69–75.

Ross, S. H. (1989). Parts, wholes, and place value: A developmental review. *Arithmetic Teacher, 36*, 47–51.

Saxe, G. B. (1981). Body parts as numerals: A developmental analysis of numeration among the Oksapmin in Papua New Guinea. *Child Development, 52*, 306–316.

Schoenfeld, A. H. (1988). When good teaching leads to bad results: The disasters of "well-taught" mathematics courses. *Educational Psychologist, 23*, 145–166.

Schütte, S. (2004). Rechenwegsnotation und Zahlenblick als Vehikel des Aufbaus flexibler Rechenkompetenzen [Notation of calculation processes and number sense as a vehicle to develop flexible arithmetic competencies]. *Journal für Mathematik-Didaktik, 25*(2), 130–148.

Schwartz, J. (1988). Intensive quantity and referent transforming arithmetic operations. In J. Hiebert & M. Behr (Eds.), *Number concepts and operations in the middle grades* (pp. 41–52). Hillsdale, NJ: Erlbaum.

Schwebel, A. I., & Schwebel, C. R. (1974). The relationship between performance on Piagetian tasks and impulsive responding. *Journal for Research in Mathematics Education, 5*(2), 98–104.

Selter, C. (2001). Addition and subtraction of three-digit numbers: German elementary children's success, methods and strategies. *Educational Studies in Mathematics, 47*(2), 145–173.doi:10.1023/A:1014521221809

Selter, C. (2009). Creativity, flexibility, adaptivity, and strategy use in mathematics. *ZDM: The International Journal on Mathematics Education, 41*(5), 619–625.

Seron, X., & Fayol, M. (1994). Number transcoding in children: A functional analysis. *British Journal of Developmental Psychology, 12*, 281–300.

Shulman, L. S. (1986). Those who understand: Knowledge growth in teaching. *Educational Researcher, 15*, 4–14.

Silver, E. (1976). Relations among Piagetian grouping structures: A training study. *Journal for Research in Mathematics Education, 7*(5), 308–314.

Simon, M. A. (1993). Prospective elementary teachers' knowledge of division. *Journal for Research in Mathematics Education, 24*, 233–254.

Simon, M. A., & Schifter, D. (1991). Towards a constructivist perspective: An intervention study of mathematics teacher development. *Educational Studies in Mathematics, 22*(4), 309–331.

Singer, J. A, Kohn, A. S, & Resnick, L. B. (1997). Knowing about proportions in different contexts. In T. Nunes & P. Bryant (Eds.), *Learning and teaching mathematics. An international perspective* (pp. 115–132). Hove (UK): Psychology Press.

Song, M. J., & Ginsburg, H. P. (1988). The effect of the Korean number system on young children's counting: A natural experiment in numerical bilingualism. *International Journal of Psychology, 23*, 319–332.

Sparks, B. E., Brown, J. A., & Bassler, O. C. (1970). The feasibility of inducing number conservation through training on reversibility. *Journal for Research in Mathematics Education, 1*(3), 134–143.

Sriraman, B., & English, L. (2010). *Theories of mathematics education: Seeking new frontiers.* Berlin: Springer.

Star, J. R., & Newton, K. J. (2009). The nature and development of experts' strategy flexibility for solving equations. *ZDM: The International Journal on Mathematics Education, 41*(5), 557–567.

Steffe, L. (1994). Children's multiplying schemes. In G. Harel & J. Confrey (Eds.), *The development of multiplicative reasoning in the learning of mathematics* (pp. 3–40). Albany, NY: State University of New York Press.

Steffe, L. P., & Carey, R. L. (1972). Equivalence and order relations as interrelated by four- and five-year-old children. *Journal for Research in Mathematics Education, 3*(2), 77–88.

Steffe, L. P., & Thompson, P. W. (2000). Radical constructivism in action: building on the pioneering work of Ernst von Glasersfeld. New York Falmer.

Stern, E. (1993). What makes certain arithmetic word problems involving the comparison of sets so difficult for children? *Journal of Educational Psychology, 85*, 7–23.

Streefland, L. (1984). Search for the roots of ratio: Some thoughts on the long term learning process (Towards…A Theory): Part I: Reflections on a teaching experiment. *Educational Studies in Mathematics, 15*, 327–348.

Streefland, L. (1985). Search for the roots of ratio: Some thoughts on the long term learning process (Towards…A Theory): Part II: The outline of the long Term learning process. *Educational Studies in Mathematics, 16*, 75–94.

Streefland, L. (1987). *How to teach fractions so as to be useful.* Utrecht, The Netherlands: The State University of Utrecht.

Streefland, L. (1991). Fractions, an integrated perspective. In L. Streefland (Ed.), *Realistic mathematics education in primary school* (pp. 93–118). Utrecht: Freudenthal Institute, Utrecht University.

Streefland, L. (1997). Charming fractions or fractions being charmed? In T. Nunes & P. Bryant (Eds.), *Learning and teaching mathematics. An international perspective* (pp. 347–372). Hove, UK: Psychology Press.

Svenson, O., & Broquist, S. (1975). Strategies for solving simple addition problems. *Scandinavian Journal of Psychology, 16*, 143–151.

Taloumis, T. (1975). the relationship of area conservation to area measurement as affected by sequence of presentation of Piagetian area tasks to boys and girls in grades one through three. *Journal for Research in Mathematics Education, 6*(4), 232–242.

Taloumis, T. (1979). Scores on Piagetian area tasks as predictors of achievement in mathematics over a four-year period. *Journal for Research in Mathematics Education, 10*(2), 120–134.

Tchoshanov, M. A. (2011). Relationship between teacher knowledge of concepts and connections, teaching practice, and student achievement in middle grades mathematics. *Educational Studies in Mathematics, 76*(2), 141–164.

Thompson, P. W. (1993). Quantitative reasoning, complexity, and additive structures. *Educational Studies in Mathematics, 3*, 165–208.

Thompson, P. (1994). The development of the concept of speed and its relationship to concepts of rate. In G. Harel & J. Confrey (Eds.), *The development of multiplicative reasoning in the learning of mathematics* (pp. 181–236). Albany, New York: State University of New York Press.

Thompson, I. (1999). Mental calculation strategies for addition and subtraction Part 1. *Mathematics in School,* November, 2–4.

Thompson, I. (2000). Teaching Place Value in the UK: time for a reappraisal? *Educational Review, 52*(3), 291–298.

Threlfall, J. (2002). Flexible mental calculation. *Educational Studies in Mathematics, 50*(1), 29–47.

Threlfall, J. (2009). Strategies and flexibility in mental calculation. *ZDM: The International Journal on Mathematics Education, 41*(5), 541–555.

Tirosh, D. (2000). Enhancing prospective teachers' knowledge of children's conceptions: The case of division of fractions. *Journal for Research in Mathematics Education, 31*(1), 5–25.

Tirosh, D., & Graeber, A. O. (1989). Preservice elementary teachers' explicit beliefs about multiplication and division. *Educational Studies in Mathematics, 20*(1), 79–96.

Tirosh, D., & Graeber, A. O. (1990). Evoking cognitive conflict to explore preservice teachers' thinking about division. *Journal for Research in Mathematics Education*, 98–108.

Tirosh, D., Even, R., & Robinson, N. (1998). Simplifying algebraic expressions: Teacher awareness and teaching approaches. *Educational Studies in Mathematics, 35*(1), 51–64.

Toluk-Uçar, Z. (2009). Developing pre-service teachers understanding of fractions through problem posing.*Teaching and Teacher Education, 25*(1), 166–175.

Torbeyns, J., De Smedt, B., Ghesquière, P., & Verschaffel, L. (2009a). Jump or compensate? Strategy flexibility in the number domain up to 100. *ZDM: The International Journal on Mathematics Education, 41*(5), 581–590.

Torbeyns, J., De Smedt, B., Stassens, N., Ghesquière, P., & Verschaffel, L. (2009b). Solving subtraction problems by means of indirect addition. *Mathematical Thinking and Learning, 11*(1–2), 79–91.

Torbeyns, J., Ghesquière, P., & Verschaffel, L. (2009c). Efficiency and flexibility of indirect addition in the domain of multi-digit subtraction. *Learning and Instruction, 19*(1), 1–12.

Torbeyns, J., De Smedt, B., Peters, G., Ghesquière, P., & Verschaffel L. (2011). Use of indirect addition in adults' mental subtraction in the number domain up to 1,000. *British Journal of Psychology, 102*, 585–597. doi: 10.1111/j.2044-8295.2011.02019.x

Treffers, A. (1991). Didactical background of a mathematics programm for primary education. In L. Streefland (Ed.), *Realistic mathematics education in primary school* (pp. 21–56). Utrecht: Freudenthal Institute, Utrecht University.

Tsamir, P., Sheffer, R., & Tirosh, D. (2000). Intuitions and undefined operations: The case of division by zero. *Focus on Learning Problems in Mathematics, 22*(1), 1–16.

Vamvakoussi, X., & Vosniadou, S. (2004). Understanding the structure of the set of rational numbers: A conceptual change approach. *Learning and Instruction, 14*, 453–467.

Van Den Brink, J., & Streefland, L. (1979). Young children (6-8): Ratio and proportion. *Educational Studies in Mathematics, 10*, 403–420.

Van den Brink, J. (1991). Realistic arithmetic education for young children. In L. Streefland (Ed.), *Realistic mathematics education in primary school* (pp. 77–92). Utrecht: Freudenthal Institute, Utrecht University.

Van den Heuvel-Panhuizen, M. (2008). Learning from "Didactikids": An impetus for revisiting the empty number line. *Mathematics Education Research Journal, 20*(3), 6–31.

Van Hiele, P. M. (1999). Developing geometric thinking through activities that begin with play. *Teaching Children Mathematics, 5*(6), 310–316.

Van Meter, P., & Garner, J. (2005). The promise and practice of learner-generated drawing: Literature review and synthesis. *Educational Psychology Review, 17*(4), 285–325.

Vergnaud, G. (1979). The acquisition of arithmetical concepts. *Educational Studies in Mathematics, 10*, 263–274.

Vergnaud, G. (1982). A classification of cognitive tasks and operations of thought involved in addition and subtraction problems. In T. P. Carpenter, J. M. Moser & T. A. Romberg (Eds.), *Addition and subtraction: A cognitive perspective* (pp. 60–67). Hillsdale (NJ): Lawrence Erlbaum.

Vergnaud, G. (1983). Multiplicative structures. In R. Lesh & M. Landau (Eds.), *Acquisition of mathematics concepts and processes* (pp. 128–175). London: Academic Press.

Vergnaud, G. (2009). The theory of conceptual fields. *Human Development, 52*, 83–94.

Verschaffel, L. (1994). Using retelling data to study elementary school children's representations and solutions of compare problems. *Journal for Research in Mathematics Education, 25*, 141–165.

Verschaffel, L., Torbeyns, J., De Smedt, B., Luwel, K. & van Dooren, W. (2007). Strategy flexibility in children with low achievement in mathematics. *Educational and Child Psychology, 24*(2), 16–27.

Verschaffel, L., Luwel, K., Torbeyns, J., & Van Dooren, W. (2009). Conceptualizing, investigating, and enhancing adaptive expertise in elementary mathematics education. *European Journal of Psychology of Education, 24*(3), 335–359.

Verschaffel, L., Van Dooren, W., Greer, B., & Mukhopadhyay, S. (2010). Reconceptualising word problems as exercises in mathematical modelling. *Journal für Mathematik-Didaktik, 31*, 9–29.

Verschaffel, L., Torbeyns, J., Peters, G., De Smedt, B., & Ghesquière, P. (2016). *The astonishing efficacy of the addition by subtraction strategy in the number domain up to 1000—results of a choice/no-choice study with children.* Paper presented at the ICME-13, Hamburg, 23–31 July.

Von Glasersfeld, E. (1981). An attentional model for the conceptual construction of units and number. *Journal for Research in Mathematics Education, 12*, 83–94.

Wheeler, M., & Feghali, I. (1983). Much ado about nothing: Preservice elementary school teachers' concept of zero. *Journal of Research in mathematics Education, 14*(3), 147–155.

Willis, G. B., & Fuson, K. C. (1988). Teaching children to use schematic drawings to solve addition and subtraction word problems. *Journal of Educational Psychology, 80*(2), 192–201.

Young, R. M., & O'Shea, T. (1981). Errors in children's subtraction. *Cognitive Science, 5*, 153–177.

Zaslavsky, C. *Africa counts: Number and pattern in African cultures.* Chicago Review Press, 1999.